AGING IS A PART OF THE JOURNEY

CORRINE A LUND

Copyright © 2023

Corrine A Lund

All rights reserved.

ISBN: 979-8-89075-508-7

I would like to share a special story with you before I continue writing the rest of my book. The story is cute in itself, but it also contains a message that fits especially well for our aging adventure.

We are friends with a couple, Jane and Perry, who are very dear to us. They recently moved out of the house where they had lived for fifty-three years to be close to their adult children. Jane shared this story about their young daughter. Before I continue with my book, I would like to share her story.

When this little girl was two years old, she needed encouragement with her potty training. Young people today probably don't remember a country star from the Grand Ole Opry. Minnie Pearl was her name and her trademark was a large straw hat with the price tag hanging from the brim. Even though 'the hat' was an important part of Minnie Pearl's image, somehow the words "Minnie Pearl wears big girl pants" also contained a humorous description of this famous lady. That was all the motivation this little girl needed to spur her to successfully finish potty training.

Our friend's daughter enjoyed visiting her rather elegant grandmother. While sitting on a red velvet stool on one particular visit, this child forgot about the 'big girl pants,' and the red velvet cushion became a very wet cushion. She and her momma were embarrassed by the incident, but the grandmother wasn't. This elderly lady put her arm around the little girl's mother and shared this priceless life lesson in just a few words.

"Honey," she said, "Things are to use. People are to love. Don't ever get that confused!"

These words have remained with my friend through all these years. Now it is time for them to consider all the things they have accumulated during their many years of married life. My friend reminded me that as they move to a new and different home, they are moving with what they love– each other. We don't love 'things' even if we have had them for so many years. We love the people who have made our life what it is today and the connections we have built along the way. Those are the people who are the gold nuggets in our lives.

And now, I will move on to my story. Tuck that bit of wisdom deep into your heart and soul and remember the importance of those words. We enjoy the things that surround us and share the memories of so many experiences but remember.

"Honey, things are to use. People are to love."

Introduction

And so, my thoughts begin.

Throughout my life, I have approached the concept of aging with a bit of humor. It's going to happen. Why not enjoy it? I haven't always been this old. As my hair started to turn gray, my husband commented, "There are women who would pay a lot of money to have hair the color of yours!" I just smiled.

I always enjoyed the compliment, "You certainly don't look your age!" Thank you very much, but I do realize that I am growing older. I wasn't given an owner's manual so that I might look ahead for directions regarding this aging process. Although, I would guess that one might find such a thing on YOUTUBE! I suppose I might be a bit naïve about growing older. I go through periods when I feel like I am on top of all the important things I need to know to proceed on this aging path. Important documents. Have we created end-of-life directions for our family? Do they know where all the important papers are filed? Have we saved telephone contacts and passwords in an organized manner?

And what about financial planning? We have been careful planners over the years, but important information must be considered. There are so many significant considerations regarding one's finances! Health care is probably the one concern at the forefront of the minds of anyone with gray hair. Can I afford it? All of these are important, and when I talk with friends my age, it seems we pretty much all have the same concerns.

And then there is the challenging part of getting life in order. "How will we ever get rid of all the things we have packed away in storage?" Another way to put that would be, "When is the yard sale?" The younger generation is too practical to be interested in the fine china we cherish and only use on special holidays. And they can't be put into the dishwasher!

What about all those toys tucked away in box after box? Who is going to want all the toys saved from days when the kids were little? I saved our grandson's Batman collection with so many toys for such a long time, and then I realized that I was saving that memory for me! I remember all the hours of play we had together on the floor or under the dining room table, playing with toys that didn't even need batteries.

Of course, all those "things" are important. I procrastinate. Those photos don't need to be sorted out today. I can go through the boxes in the basement later. I procrastinate, and I must not do that any longer. These are things that should have been considered yesterday! It is the "winter season" of my life, and I think, "This is going to be a piece of cake!" I'm not sure that is true! I hope the need to understand, accept, and be aware of all that is a part of the aging process and then attempt to manage all that needs to be done on an ongoing basis.

It is a beautiful, clear, sunshiny day as I am writing this morning. One of those picture-perfect winter days. I have been working on the plans, layout, and topics for this book for some time. What is it that I would like you, the reader, to find unique and helpful as I share stories related to my remembering? Might there be some ideas you can use or maybe something brings a smile as you say, "I sure can relate to that!" I do not want you to be fearful of these "gray hair/ forgetting where things are" experiences because you and I can make the aging process as positive as we are able, even if we need the assistance of others. This winter season is a gift! Get out your "winter" memories. We are about to explore the aging adventure.

Aging is challenging because we have not done this before. Aging is challenging because some of us do it for various lengths of time and with assorted health situations. We even do it in different places. What I need is the assurance that what I am going through during this time in my life is just how this is meant to be for me.

I would also like to encourage you to travel with other aging people. No, I don't mean that literally. I mean that it is helpful to support each other and to be there for each other as we explore this unfamiliar path. Laugh together. Share some stories. Grieve together and share tears. Be generous with your hugs. Aging is not like a board game where there is competition as to who is going to win. We are all in this one to help each other. Think of it as all of us being winners who have been blessed with life in our unique ways. Life is a blessing to be lived, learned, and loved – each of us on our journey.

I thought about my personal aging experiences. Celebrating the joys of retirement, feeling frustrated as I became aware that driving on a rainy, night has become a challenge, falling asleep in the middle of the chapter of an exciting book, or not having the energy to complete all my tasks in one day. Did I think that I would experience aging behaving as the character of Wonder Woman?

This book is not a medical journal with scientific facts regarding aging. It is not a psychological journal article about why we feel the way we do as we grow older (often written by a much younger person!) My sharing is for ordinary people like you and me who are approaching the winter season of life and would like to carry on in the best way possible.

I have left some pages blank, not because I forgot to write on them, but because I would like to invite you to write on them. The blank pages are for you and your thoughts. Write. Make notes of things to do. Lay out a plan for some particular task that needs to be done. Read with a pencil in your hand!

And now, I would like to invite you to explore this path together—just you and me.

***

Acknowledgments

Thank you to all those who are aging with me, providing me with what it is that I need along this path. Thank you, Jane, Daryl, Perry, Laurel, Gayle, John, Karen, and Sharon.

Thank you to my family, who once again encouraged me to take a pencil and write for others. My family is most patient.

When I say, "Would you please read this just one more time," they respond, "Sure." For that, I am most appreciative. And in the meantime, as I sit at the computer well past the dinner hour, my husband patiently suggests, "Let's do carryout tonight!" You are all a much-loved blessing!

And it seems appropriate to thank all the medical professionals who have done so much to keep/make me healthy. Another hip replacement and I am ready for a good hike!

Thank you to all the people who are guiding me at Excel Book Publishers - People I know only by their voice or their email. I hope I don't give you gray hair in the process of getting this all together! You have been helpful and patient

Thank you to all those who are aging with me, providing me with what it is that I need along this path.

Dedication

Carolyn, in your memory

For all the good times we spent together

For the funny secrets we shared and laughed about

And then, the last time we were together you said to me "I might not see you again."

Carolyn, you left this earthly life too soon.

Lord,

It's me. One of your 'older children'

Do you mean it?

Really?

When you say that you will accept me just as I am?

Some days that seems difficult to believe.

Lord,

You have done so much for me.

I often have more requests than thank-you's

But please. Just one more thing.

Explain something to me about this 'Just as I am' stuff.

Lord,

Some days I am simply frustrated, afraid, and lonely. Why would you be interested in me when I am feeling so confused?

You even send your invitation when I am in a complaining mood. I look pretty comfortable on the outside, but I can be quite a mess on the inside. There seem to be challenges within me, and I can't figure out which side is winning. Sometimes I feel young and full of energy, but I look in the mirror and change my mind. I tripped over the design on the kitchen floor!

Some days I feel as though I have lost my way. I forget the simplest of things, and then I end up worrying about why I didn't remember.

Some days I feel angry when I can't control what is happening. The ceiling seems to be falling in on me. Oh, it isn't that bad, but I don't like not having control over these little things.

Do you want me to come just as I am?

I do remember that you said I am the apple of your eye. Surely that must mean something special!

[Keep me as the apple of your eye; hide me in the shadow of your wings – Psalm 17:8.]

I look forward to joy-filled days when I remember all the blessings you have showered on me. You understand me without confronting me.

That is comforting, indeed.

I will remind you that you said I was your child and even invited me to your house, just as I am. There is also the promise of a place just for me in your house, and you also promised to keep the door open.

Lord,

Seriously, this is one invitation that I am going to remember.

Thank you from the deepest part of my heart!

It was so very long ago. The world began, and it continued. There was dark and light, creatures and vegetation, rocks and water.

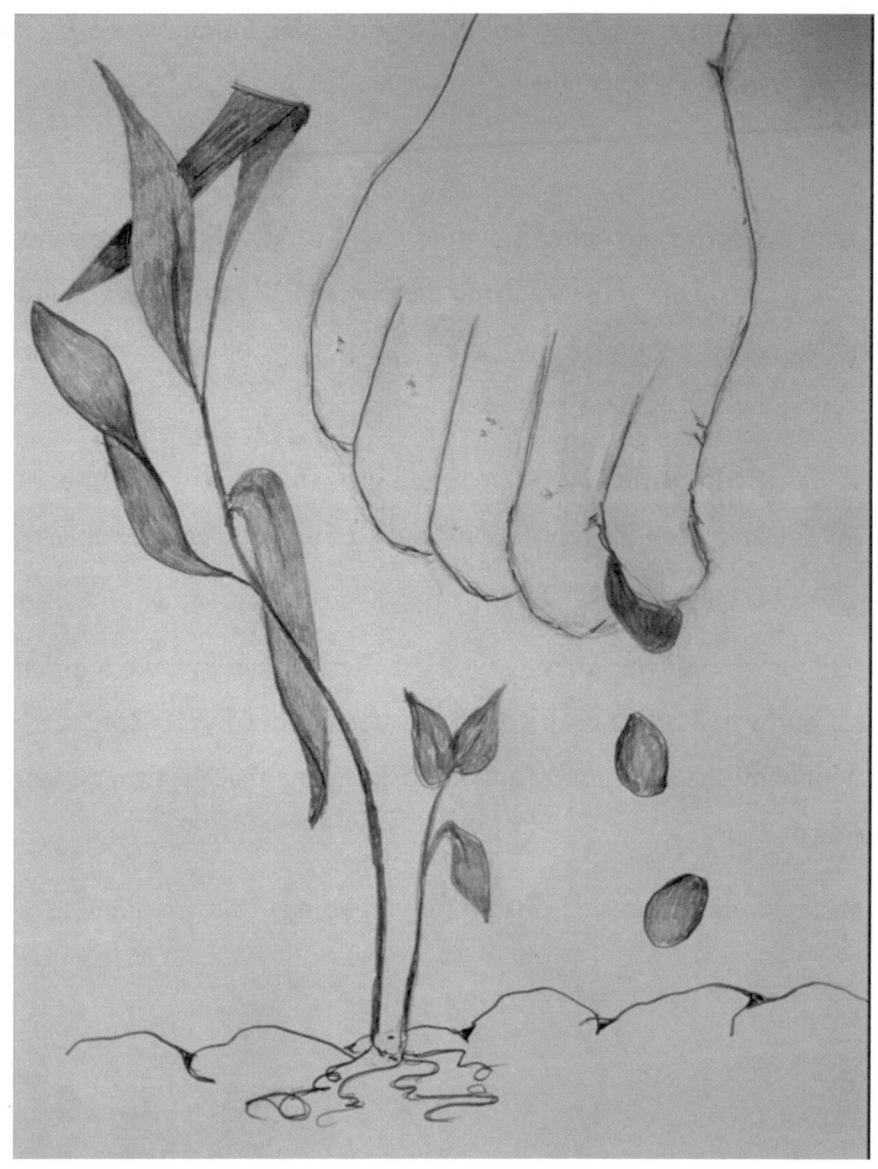

My own story began a long time ago

Two things seem similar when addressing the longevity of the world and my longevity. There was a beginning for both - a '**Process**…' And the world continues to age just as I do. The process continues. Both the world and I are part of a process.

One day it began, and the process continued. Like a new seed in the ground, watered by the rain and warmed by the sun, it grows. Then one day, there is a shoot peaking its greenery out of the rich soil. It grows and blooms until the blossom falls from the plant one day and drops the seed onto the earth again. But the story doesn't end. The process continues seed after seed, day after day, year after year. And story after story.

I grow older slowly but surely, and after me, others will follow. Each day promises some kind of adventure. Each year provides another piece to the process. We each have unique stories and adventures, and the process continues. I am sharing my story, but even after the last words have been read, somehow, the journey will continue.

Together we will experience joy and grief, loss and growth. We will remember together, and we might even forget some parts of the story. Some days I feel quite comfortable with the unknown; I would appreciate your insight on others.

Hold my hand and remember your journey with me. Remember how we burst into the world and gradually worked our way through each one of the steps of our lives? Hold my hand, and I will move forward with confidence, strength, and hope, knowing that the process will continue as long as the world continues.

Join me as we share our adventures on this journey of aging. Take my hand as we begin the walk together.

Hands

Hands to help me stand up. Hands to help me walk with you.

Lend me a hand, please. Can you give me a hand with that?

Hands reach out to greet me, and then one day, those same hands will wave goodbye and hopefully, will throw a kiss in my direction.

I can help you- put your hand in mine.

Sometimes I need a strong hand,

A hand that is not afraid to reach out to what it is that I need.

Sometimes it is my hand that is strong, reaching out to help others.

Into your hands, O Lord, I put my fears and worries.

Hold me up, O Lord, lend me a hand on this journey of growing older.

For this, I am most appreciative. Thank you, Lord.

Process – continuing, ongoing, without an ending.

Each moment of life is a piece in the whole process. Sometimes it is difficult to understand, but we need to try. Maybe it just happens.

It is how we live our life that is significant!" And this, he adds, is what the meaning of life is; as we stop to reflect on our growing older years.

Process – ON-GOING. Do I know where it began or even how it began? How can I begin to anticipate an ending to this process?

Process – It is not the same for everyone or everything. We begin and continue to grow through this process day by day. Slowly we begin, and slowly we grow, learning, exploring, and experimenting. Think of the times we discovered something new. So many experiences begin with just one step.

__Give my life meaning__...as shared by Daryl, another aging senior. That age-old question had taken him far too many years to come to some clarity about what this life is all about. He shared that he is now clear about at least one thing: when his life is over, many of the things that he had been preoccupied with no longer matter. What worried and kept his attention in his 30's, 40's, and 50's just weren't all that important. What does it matter how I look or where I live, or what kind of job I held…But he is clear about the importance of his family and the unconditional love they share. He observed that when he and his wife were young parents, in many ways, they were still kids themselves. They did their best, but it was 'on-the-job' training that helped them through the years of raising their children.

And what does he want to pass on to his children…the next generation? The hope is that they learn about life more quickly than he did. That it is not all the 'best of everything' that their children need but the deep love that is shared in a family. And he adds, "I hope my compassion, sensitivity, sincerity, integrity, authenticity – my character and not my competence is what mattered. It was my wisdom, not my success or lack thereof. As we are on this journey, it is the meaning of life, as we stop to reflect on our growing older years.

PROCESS - ON GOING. Do I even know where to begin or even how it all began. How can I begin to anticipate an end to this process?

PROCESS - It is not the same for everyone or everything. We begin and continue to grow through this process day by day. Slowly we begin and slowly we grow, learning, exploring, and experimenting.

As we are on the journey of aging, a day at a time, it sometimes as though we are just testing the waters. But, at other times it might feel as though we made a very big splash!

We learn that the most difficult experiences are done more easily when approached and explored with the help and wisdom of others.

Sometimes it seems that the most important part of the process is simply sitting still, listening to what the quiet has to say to us.

We travel through spring and summer, and soon autumn begins to encourage us to a time of rest. A quiet time of reflecting as we look back as well as ponder what the future holds.

It might be a surprise as winter arrives. Winter has a way of sneaking up on us, and even with the beauty of new fallen snow, it can be a challenge.

Some experiences seem to go on for such a long time…like winter, for instance. But in the process, there is hope and the promise of new life. Even with hope and the promises that we are loved and cared for, sometimes it feels as though we are just hanging on. We must learn to trust the process as well as those who love and care for us. It's normal if winter seems long and cold and a bit lonely. Remember, in that deep winter, we can find strength as well as gentleness.

Long, cold, and lonely. Frightening. Winter can be challenging. As though we are just hanging on, but through the pain, we slowly open ourselves to forgiveness. Another life story from an aging senior.

A childhood secret, unknown even to her young self, but she was being held captive by a grey cloud that was devouring her inner being. Even with the hidden pain, it took multiple personal traumatic events years later for the dark secrets to surface. So many tragic events, one after another, until she was mentally broken, and her emotional health hit bottom. After experiencing deep despair and severe depression, she slowly drew on her faith and the help of a psychotherapist. With this support and guidance, she came to understand and open herself to the immense relief that forgiveness could provide. Forgiveness would be the key to her recovery. It was being open to allowing forgiveness that gave her the freedom to embrace her true self, which allowed her to move on with her life.

Remembering and forgetting. Remembering can also open the doors to the most painful of experiences. We might think that forgetting is the only way to walk through these dark times. Deciding that forgetting or not being able to remember may just make the dark even darker.

Strength came through her deep faith and provided the building blocks that she needed to become the person she is today. Yesterday, today, and tomorrow, are all critical to recovering from the trauma that life can put on our path. She adds one thought: Forgiving does not necessarily mean forgetting, but it does allow for the healing of old scars and the ability to move forward with a meaningful life.

(A story bravely shared and a story that explored the darkness that can cause us to feel as though we are just hanging on. As we grow into our older years, it becomes impossible to move forward as we carry secrets and trauma. Recovery with forgiveness cleared the path for her and allowed the tomorrows to be healthy and whole. The years ahead no longer were times when she felt that she was just holding on. As we grow older, it is never too late to learn how to refill our hearts and soul)

The autumn seeds have dropped into the earth. Some seeds have been blown by the wind. Parts of the winter season can seem difficult and the promise of new growth might seem impossible

The dance goes on, and the process continues. Of course, there are tricks along the way. Things for which we did not plan. The process goes off in a direction we had not expected. Winter seems long. If we have the patience and willingness to endure, each step will eventually bring new and amazing growth.

And the key to the process…

Time. One season after another.

Slowly but persistently.

If we hold tight to patience, we will discover the process is leading us with gentle wisdom and strength. We each must learn the process appropriate for our individual journey.

Days begin. The evening comes.

Be open to ideas, encouragement, and support. It is not good to stand alone, pretending to be strong.

A journey begins quietly with a fragile new life, cautiously and carefully, and sometimes life ends in the same way. We just don't know exactly how we are going to walk our path.

Watch nature as it becomes the timekeeper, the calendar, and the clock.

The process may seem demanding, overwhelming, and powerful. Nature's gentle creatures seem ready to follow the dance, and that can guide us to pay attention. They probably have something to teach us.

Listen to the music. Pay attention as the winds blow new beginnings your way. Nature teaches us how to smooth the rough edges.

And what do we do while we work at paying attention?

We learn to follow the path most suited for us.

We move forward with determination, with a purpose that will fill our hearts and soul.

It might be winter, but we still can hear the music.

LISTENING AND LEARNING...

And as we grow older, if we listen carefully, that music can bring a smile as we relate to circumstances in the lives of other 'seniors.'

A friend shares a humorous story about his church's decision to provide supplies to mothers of newborn children. His wife sent him to the store in search of diapers. Now, his grandchildren are almost all grown, so it had been some time since he had made such a search. He looked around, and after some time, he finally gave in to asking for some assistance. "Diapers?" The assistant in the store replied. "They would be in aisle J6." He thought, "No wonder I couldn't find them. I have been wandering in everything from the pharmacy to the garments aisle and to areas that seemed to be selling car seats that resembled those used in a space launch. And his wandering continued as he searched for aisle J6. He smiled as he looked up at the label on the wall where he was searching, and to his surprise...there they were...the shelf with the boxes of Depends!

And the music continues with the loving story of Tessy. She was a professional clown with a heart! The joy of reaching out to children as a gentle clown began many years ago, but Tessy continued her performances until the children began to call her Grandma Tessy. Tessy had a calling, relating to children in a way in which her appearance as a clown in makeup didn't frighten them. Slowly she applied her makeup in front of her young audience so that they knew the real Tessy was still under all the exaggeration of the clown's appearance. For many years she showed her love and enthusiasm with young children. Her performance was never loud and boisterous, but rather, she shared in a manner that brought laughter and fun to the children so they could relate to her character without fear.

Clowns are an example of how we can be confused by appearance. People like Tessy touched so many children with her love, and the special thing about Tessy is that she continued her 'act' long into her senior years. She was a gift to the children, and for years Tessy brought smiles to the kids. Of course, we need to be wary of appearance, but how often do we judge others by how they 'appear' to us. Look deeper. Remember Tessy and her gentle approach as she became her jolly character. Tessy, the clown, followed a beautiful path as it led her all the way to being Grandma Tessy.

Growing older is quite a story but it is also 'real life.' And for sure, growing older is a process. It seems to be a cycle that goes on and on. I have given a lot of thought to beginnings. Siblings and parents, grandparents and great-grandparents. Dates for birth, weddings, and deaths. Beginnings and endings with life sandwiched in between. We all start somewhere, and then that beginning is followed up with us 'doing' something, and when we are through with all of that, we stop and look back at all that has happened.

Looking back and remembering opens the door for us to pass the baton on to the next generation, and then– Guess what? What? It starts all over again. Confusing? I guess it could be, but this simply is the process by which we are all active participants. The door is opened, over and over again, until the boards are worn, and the handle barely hangs on. But the door always remains, waiting for the next generation, the next person, to open it yet another time.

Life begins again and again.

So many pieces to the process. New life begins. A house is built for a new family. A garden is planted, and a field is tilled. The baby grows older, and the parents grow older. Is there anything that isn't growing?

So what is unique about this ongoing process of growing, whether it is the seeds that are planted in the rich garden soil or that new life that begins step by step on his or her journey?

I remember the rows and rows of jars of home-canned fruit and vegetables in the basement storage area in the old farmhouse where I grew up. I remember picking strawberries out of the patch that the wandering moose also thought was tasty. (Remember, I grew up in northern Minnesota.) All that produce provided the fixings for wonderful home-cooked meals.

I remember first grade. I remember riding my bicycle on the country roads with my friends. I remember birthday parties—a lot of them. What I wasn't thinking about then was 'growing older.' Growing older was happening rather quietly.

Then the day came when my mother could not plant her garden, and my father could no longer drive the tractor. Days passed. Then came the days when they could no longer live on the farm. I remembered all their years together, working on what was important to them.

I was following in their path, living my life journey as they had lived theirs. Well, sort of. I was growing older, but the funny thing is, I don't remember when it all started for me. I was no longer young but not yet old. I still remember the garden with the rows of produce and the wheat fields blowing in the Minnesota autumn wind.

And then there did come a day when I realized that something was different. Changes. There were gray streaks in my hair that were not put there by a hairstylist. My knees ached when the weather changed. Sometimes I forget things like where I put my reading glasses. As I was more cognizant of the changes, recognizing that there indeed were changes, I began to consider what this all meant. I thought that maybe I was getting a bit older, but I didn't know how that could be happening.

So I thought about what was happening, and yes, indeed, life was a bit different. I would sometimes sit quietly, thinking and remembering. I remembered many things and wondered what might be ahead. I quickly became aware that it was much easier to look back and remember than to think about the unknown.

I thought about what was happening right now. New experiences. Gradually that space between being young and becoming older was beginning to make a bit of sense to me. A voice deep within encouraged me to think of this journey as a gift. A gift with surprises. Maybe there would be challenges that might cause some stumbles, but I can do it. Indeed, I can do this aging thing. The voice reminded me to be aware of the moment and soak up the blessings. Reach out to others for support. Find love in the moment and live each day to fill my soul. Filling my soul to overflowing!

I thought. Maybe aging is like the frosting on the cake. The last step in creating a wonderful, delicious life. As I enjoy the frosting on my cake, someone else is just beginning to decide what flavor they would like for their cake. So many different stages – sifting the flour, tasting the batter, decorating, and finally adding the frosting.

I thought, "Now that was one delicious cake!"

AND GOD SAID TO JEREMIAH,

"I will be with you from the beginning to the end. I will be there every day and I will show you the way. If you have any questions, don't be afraid to ask me. I have a plan just for you and I know what it is that I am doing. I am going to take care of you for the whole journey."

AND SO, IT IS.

I recently found an entry in a journal I had written several years ago.

During all those many months, I wrote and created. When I wasn't writing, I was making something; when I wasn't creating, I was writing. As challenging as this whole process proved to be, the medical choices we all made together seemed to work. My physicians and support team were angels on my path, and my family and friends were amazing gifts from my Creator God. My body was healing, but I needed something more to comfort my heart and soul.

One day a thought popped up in my mind. (My husband and daughter take credit for the idea)! After all the writing I had been doing, why not combine all those words and create a book?

Writing a book would just mean organizing all the words I had already written. After my experiences of meeting others on the same journey, I knew I was not the only one with questions and fears, wondering about the unknown. I decided to put all those thoughts together, imagining I was conversing with others on a similar journey.

This became a journey of faith, a journey of learning about acceptance, a time to understand patience with the unknown, an opportunity to look fear straight on, and then eventually to celebrate joy. And that is just what I did. I concluded that the very last story in

God Blessed Them for the Journey, my first book where I included the story of the feather, will remain a surprise…with the hope you might want to read it. Feathers continue to provide a means by which I am made aware of what it is that I need to pay attention to whatever that might be. It always seems to speak to my heart. At that time, that was my story.

Today I am in the midst of a new story, a new journey. That previous experience was about illness and the search for wholeness. We all meet challenges throughout our lives, unique as each one of us is. The cancer story quickly expanded to reach so many different individual or personal concerns. Kids might be bullied or abused, an experience that could continue to create wounds that could last a lifetime. Young adults might face a world where hopes and dreams sometimes fall between the cracks. We all suffer loss in a million different ways. We know what brokenness feels like, even though we may not know how to mend it. So many challenges were on my mind as I wrote.

And then, after many months of healing from my cancer experience, I was once again a healthy, busy wife and mother. I slowly began to feel a sense of peace and acceptance with even more energy. I continued writing and creating, but now both had a new meaning for me—a purpose. I didn't need to prove anything with either my artwork or my writing. What I was doing was filling my heart and soul for me! That was like a continuation of my own 'healing treatments.'

That all happened over twenty years ago. I still watch for feathers on my path. May I share an example that puts a smile on my face?

I am currently recovering from a total hip replacement. My husband was preparing the car for an early morning drive to surgery, and I was waiting just outside the door. There was a covering over the entryway where I was standing, and for some reason, I glanced upward, and guess what. There was, slowly floating down, a very tiny white feather. No, there were no birds around to send me off to surgery! My husband was in the car, and I was waiting outside. I know you are wondering- yes, I kept the feather, and the surgery went wonderfully well. No, those feathers are not magic, but each feather reminds me of the moment. It just happens when one pays attention

My husband and I have retired and live in a lovely lake community which we both dearly love. Deer in the front yard and squirrels entertaining us in the back yard. Bird feeders everywhere, and a house surrounded by magnificent oak and maple trees. Our daughter and her family live just down the road, and we love that even more than the trees and the squirrels.

We are retired. We are healthy. We so much enjoy what 'lake living' offers. But we are changing. We are both growing older. We are definitely on a journey exploring a new and unknown path. Maybe this sharing of stories will somehow speak to your journey and needs.

I tease my husband about forgetting where he put his keys. He will remind me about a particular appointment. Did I remember? "Oh, I thought that was next week!" I reply and smile. We get up too frequently during the night and have been known to go to bed with a heating pad to soothe sore muscles. We are growing older, and the path ahead is not as clear as we would like. We have just been informed of another medical concern which was totally unexpected. On the drive home from the physician's office, I said to my husband, "I can't believe this. We are living 'my book!" as I write.

And with changes come new emotions that might have been hidden away. Sometimes fear creeps in undetected and rears its very challenging head. Think back to when you were a small child and thought there was a monster under the bed or a scary creature in the closet. Not until that special someone you loved and trusted assured you and even proved to you that "No, there is nothing there, but I will stay with you until you fall asleep again."

With the love and support we all need, we can manage the ghost in the closet and sweep away the monster under the bed. Most of the time. The rest of the time, we are here for each other to offer encouragement and support to help us through all the changes. So, my new journey is the journey of growing older and aging. I can think back to yesterday but can't turn back the calendar. I can take on the concerns of today, but tomorrow still waits in the unknown. My stories will not be just about those ghosts under the bed or pretending I am Wonder Woman but simply sharing the inevitable journey on the path of aging.

Of course, there are concerns. We all experience them. Once I chose this topic about which to share my stories, 'aging' has turned up everywhere. I read the new AARP magazine, and there were, of course, articles about growing older. I had to laugh because yesterday we received a 'free gift' from AARP – my encouragement to continue on my path, maybe. I listened to an excellent podcast where the presenters opened the conversation with the topic of death, which we, too often, make into the monster under the bed.

I can't change the fact that aging will be my constant companion in the days ahead. I am growing older. Fact! It seems that the face in the mirror doesn't look like mine. Well, it does, but it doesn't look how I think it should. And aging comes with a ton of concerns and questions. I might thoroughly enjoy the freedom of retirement, but I can't ignore the realities of this particular time in my life.

Whoever we are, we can't put aging on the shelf to be dealt with at some other more convenient time. Aging will not put up with being ignored! And actually, the persistence of aging does offer some excellent learning experiences. It really does. I sometimes think that I wish I had realized that years ago. Watch for your feather and pay attention. Growing older is happening even if you are not choosing to take a step to get on the path. What is important is that we understand the directions and sign markers on our path and then be willing to consider acceptance, change, frustrations, and even fear. Or maybe, especially, fear.

Life experiences have taught me what I can or cannot change and what doors might open if I am willing to take a step across the threshold. I have learned there are ways in which I can lessen the stress on my body. I understand that grief leaves a hole in one's heart that seems impossible to fill, but if I listen to those who love me, the sun may shine again. I know how angry I can become when a familiar task has become very difficult to accomplish. So do I remain in an angry state of being or am I willing to understand that there might be another way to accomplish that task?

I'm not growing younger. I understand. Or do I? My husband and I were involved in an aging conversation one evening. Yes, a real conversation. It was a conversation about forgetting. I remember a face, but I just can't remember their name. And then we talked about driving at night and other concerns about our current driving skills. (Not our favorite conversation topic!) And then into the tough stuff…what about finances. Are we good, and if so, will we continue to be good? It was one of those conversations where one thing leads to another. These conversations are important!

I am writing, this time, not about illness and the concerns that come with whatever the health concern might be. I am writing about what I simply can't stop. The words I have used previously are *'aging is inevitable.'*

Life is a series of seasons and is much like those oak and maple trees in our woods. Green buds peak through as the early spring approaches, followed by the billions of leaves that shade our house in the summer. Autumn color is amazing, and then gradually, as if these trees needed to rest, the leaves begin to fall to the ground. All as the Creator intended. I do have choices. I can enjoy the beauty of the early snowfall, but I need to remember to scatter salt on the sidewalk so I don't fall. If I remain angry with the winter, it will only wear me down, and in the end, the snow will still remain. As I refer to them, the seasons will hopefully teach me something about acceptance on this journey. My learning will deepen when I am open to understanding what is happening on my path. The learning deepens as I move toward acceptance.

I sometimes dread going out in the winter weather, but thankfully, I can still manage the unexpected snowfalls. I am living the seasons of my life, one season at a time, and now, it is one step at a time as I explore just what winter has to offer.

Lord, help me with understanding, exploring, and accepting.

Lord,

You have known me all my days. You are with me when I awaken in the morning and when I become tired at night.

Lord,

You also are aware that my body doesn't always want to get going in the morning and that sometimes I have trouble sleeping at night.

Lord,

You have followed me throughout my entire life, or should I say you have walked in front of me to be sure my path was safe and secure.

You were with my family and me as we learned how to become a family. Now that my husband and I are just two people in a big house help us fill our days in ways that are healthy and beneficial to who we are as your children.

Lord,

During all these experiences, I have had to stop still on my path in order to recognize wrong turns to correct wrong turns. I admit that I have been stubborn, and just like a child, I often want things to go my way. You have managed to guide me, one of your children, with love and wisdom. Hopefully, I have learned to understand and accept what I have experienced on this part of my journey.

Lord,

You have stayed within my heart during those times of illness, grief, fear, and frustration. Remind me that as I have learned, I also have the responsibility to be there for others as they experience tangled roots on their path.

Lord,

You were there from the beginning. When I see a snowflake or two, remind me that winter has arrived. Be with me during this season of unknowns, this time of my life when I can feel the changes winter brings.

Lord,

Thank you for your guidance, for understanding my ups and downs on this journey. Help me remember to scatter the salt on my sidewalk. Keep me safe during my personal winter season.

Lord,

Thank you for your presence and your patience.

Please share your experience ...

Your winter season might be a bit different, so I am leaving a space for you to add your own requests to this winter prayer. Please remember there is no right or wrong way to share what is in your heart.

REMEMBERING ... AND THEN ACCEPTING CHANGE

MY STORY...

I remember when the calendar changed to the year 2000. There was a very real concern about how the world and technology, specifically, would be accepted in this new century. This kind of situation had not happened before; this step into the unknown with mind-boggling technology. This event had people around the world preparing for what they could not change or prevent from happening. Change had the world holding its breath.

The new century arrived. Midnight moved on, and it was the wee hours of the morning of the new century. I didn't feel any different, but I knew that something was different. It was an experience much like a birthday. When I awoke the following morning, the sun came up as it always does. The same thing happened when I turned sixty or seventy – very quiet steps forward, day by day, year by year, with changes that, for the most part, were not overwhelming. I continued moving forward.

As I think back, remembering some of the experiences in my life during these AARP years, I recall several truly memorable events. My father died at a young age, quite unexpectedly. My mother struggled with rheumatoid arthritis for many years. I ventured out on my own, to college, and then got married. My husband and I started our own family and learned about being a family as the circle of life continued.

Other events were happening around the world. The assassination of a President. Challenges in the political world seemed endless, as did the economic struggles. Wars. And more wars. And then 9/11...

Will humankind ever learn to live in peace? Racial issues continue to tear at the lives of countless cultures. Violence seems to be the choice of action to deal with anger. Need I continue? I remember those *big* events, both in my family and in the world.

Some memories are difficult and painful to work through. Some memories are so amazing that they still take my breath away, remembering years later. I remember visiting the Grand Canyon, all by myself, at dawn on a chilly winter morning. Looking out over that vast space left me feeling a bit overwhelmed. There was all that empty space ... empty space, but it caused me to think how filled my brain had become over my lifetime. Maybe I felt like I have filled the Grand Canyon with so many life experiences. Too much of my life has become filled to overflowing. Maybe my mental overload needs attention just like the storage area in our basement which has boxes packed with memories. My brain has become filled, much like that storage area in the basement, packed full of a multitude of things. There have just been so many things to remember

The years have passed. I remember growing up in northern Minnesota. I remember my father putting me on the large sleigh that was pulled by horses, delivering hay to the cattle. I remember so much snow in the winter that drivers would attach a small but brightly colored flag to the antennae of their cars so that others would be aware of traffic at the intersections. I remember making pizza when it was first sold in a box on the grocery shelves. The scent of my mother's bread baking in the oven was most certainly more pleasant than the scent of those first boxed pizzas.

I remember spending a summer with a family who lived in Brooklyn, New York. I seemed to constantly be amazed in a city compared to the fields of grain on the farm. I remember a storm coming up while walking the city streets of Manhattan, a yellow fury rolling down between the tall buildings. Because of the pollution in the air, the storm took on a color of its own. I also remember watching a storm approaching from miles in the distance, moving closer and closer across the open prairie, displaying an entirely different kind of fury. So many experiences. So many things I remembered.

I remember so many 'firsts' for our family. There were vacations, the birth of our daughter, and the special addition of our 'son-in-law' to our family. Then we celebrated the birth of our grandson. What can be more exciting than a squeaky clean tiny new person? I remember when we retired and began searching for our 'growing older' home. Life was moving forward, and it was constantly changing. We were changing. It didn't seem too overwhelming because it was happening slowly, one day at a time. Remember the turn of the century- could it be that it has almost been twenty-five years since then?

One day at a time. I had a haircut one day, and when I was preparing to leave, I smiled and asked the beautician to whom all that gray hair on the floor belonged. She smiled in return and said it was from the lady who had an appointment right before me. *Hmmm*. I had been her first appointment for the day!

Without a specific work schedule, retirement caused us to rely more mindfully on our calendars for day-to-day reminders. More often than not, we found ourselves asking, "Is this Thursday or Friday?" Those certainly were not the *big* things like the world events or the turn of the century, but life was changing. My husband bought a snow blower that would make removing the winter snow from the driveway easier than shoveling. We found ourselves eating out or ordering in more often. Life was changing slowly and quietly.

It seems that one needs a lifetime to understand oneself. I probably have said this many times, but that is why I have needed to live such a long time. I have so many unread books on my bookshelves, which prompts me to hope to continue living for many more years. As an artist, there are countless ideas tucked away in my head and my workroom- I need more time! Our daughter is encouraging me to record family history for both sides of our family, so I subscribed to Ancestry.com. (I kept getting that word confused with Amnesty.com). As I think about all this, I am going to need a long lifetime to accomplish my Wonder Woman plans. But plans change. Events surprise us and cause us to make unexpected changes.

My husband and I watched a movie starring Morgan Freeman. He played an angry older author who had given up on writing after the death of his wife. Alcohol took the place of his beloved typewriter. A nephew patiently tried to encourage him to change but to no avail. Change was the last thing on his playlist. Until, an inquisitive ten-year-old girl appeared at his door with lots of questions. Just what does an author do? Why don't you write if you are an author? What is an 'imagination'? Where do you get ideas for your stories? This persistent child did not give up and simply would not let Morgan Freeman's disposition and anger win. I won't give away the end of the movie. An ordinary young girl and an angry old man with an extraordinary end result. Don't tell me you can't teach an 'old dog' new tricks!

I am writing my ordinary story for ordinary readers. We can walk with each other, telling our stories that might bring either laughter or tears. We can encourage each other that it is normal to worry, to feel a bit fearful, to experience concern over what we cannot control, but all the while knowing that we are here for each other. The worries, anger, and fears need not win if we are willing to open our hearts and minds to new approaches on an unfamiliar journey. My feelings need not push me off my winter path, wishing I was thinking about spring instead of feeling the cold nip of the winds of winter.

My gold nugget to share with you- All of this journey is just as it should be. We must remember to travel the path with wisdom, understanding how to maneuver around all those tangled roots on our paths so they don't get in our way as we move forward. I am walking more slowly, but I can do it. I can learn new things and explore what this winter season has to offer.

Imagine that we are chatting about the winter weather and how we are going to manage getting around with all that snow. I wish we could sit together at the kitchen table in a warm house! I am sharing bits of my story, and since we aren't physically together, there is space for you to make notes about your stories and what you are remembering. We can think about each other, remembering and responding with "Been there…done that!" as we move from one day to the next. We can do this. Remember to watch for the feather; yes, even in the winter. We want to make this a 'pretty good winter season.'

MORE REMEMBERING…

Remembering and accepting change will continue to be key topics as we travel together. At Christmas one year, I told our grandson a story about decorating the Christmas tree when I was growing up. My grandmother lived in the country, and a fresh pine tree was cut from the woods behind her house. Yes, a live tree! The ornaments were simple, but here is the good part of the story- My grandmother had little clip-on candles. Real candles that were lit and burning. Real candles on a live tree inside her house! Can you believe that, or maybe you remember something similar from your childhood.

One more memory from childhood. I loved the Little Golden Books and paper dolls. And coloring books and crayons. I remember cutting out the Betsy McCall paper doll from the McCall magazine and then creating clothes for her. She lived in an empty shoe box decorated with colored paper. Paper dolls and new crayons. How much better can it get!

AND THAT LEADS ME TO REMEMBER SOMETHING FOR YOU TO DO...

In this empty space, remember one particular amazing childhood experience. Might it be sledding in the winter, riding your bike in the summer, or beginning first grade. Remember something that your grandchildren will respond with a "You must be kidding" kind of comment. It seems to me that some of those kinds of memories need to be recorded and remembered.

Write your own story. Make a recording. Spend time with someone you know who lives in the younger generation, telling stories that knock their socks off! If your children have no interest in those fragile china dishes, get rid of the dishes and leave wonderful stories for them instead- Memories.

We Walk Together.

AGING IS A TIME FOR REMEMBERING….

1944 was the year of my birth. My small Minnesota town had one doctor who practiced at one hospital. There was, in this community, a grocery store, a couple gas stations, several businesses, churches, and a school. I remember the grocery store with groceries on one side of the building and 'dry goods' on the other side. I often wondered, as a child, what 'dry goods' were. And then, my school – there was a large playground (at least it seemed large when I was young) with numerous pieces of equipment on which to play. I am not sure any of it would pass safety standards today! Kids could purchase ice cream after lunch. If the weather was not conducive to playing outside, the students would watch a movie in the small gymnasium.

My father was a farmer. I remember him coming in from the fields during the harvest season. Dusty and dirty from head to foot. I remember how he would carry his field dirt carefully down to the basement, where he changed clothes and cleaned up. Do you remember Lava soap?

My mother baked bread in the middle of each week. I remember the fifty pounds of flour in a cloth bag of lovely material which could later be used for something practical such as drying dishes or making an apron. The flour was dumped in a special bin in the kitchen.

I REMEMBER THE WORK THAT EACH OF THEM FOCUSED ON…TENDING TO THEIR PERSONAL TASKS. I REMEMBER.

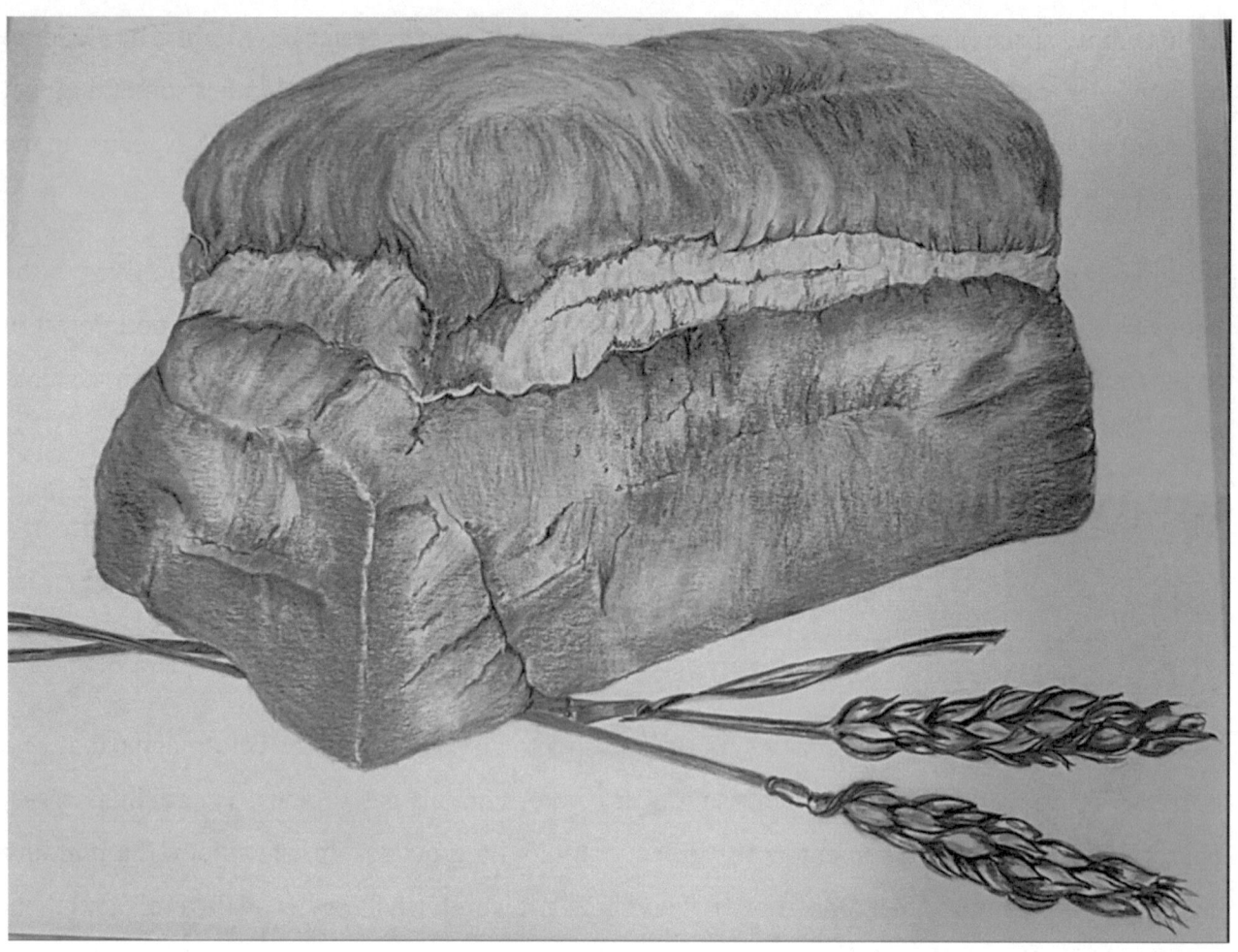

Remembering. Humankind seems to have always had the ability to remember. My dad harvested the grain he grew. My mother used flour from the wheat that had been processed from farms similar to our farm. I remember those times when I baked an occasional loaf of bread from 'scratch,' explaining to our grandson the incredible difference between homemade bread and 'store bread.'

So, with all these memories, I am inviting you to join me on the path of aging by REMEMBERING. It seems logical. A good beginning to what has been. Memories are who we have been. This is important stuff! Memories seem to be the stuffing that fills the remembering package. We share with others who it is that we and our past generations have been. Important memories because at the end of my life, my memories will be gone. Find a way to save your memories.

Stop and remember with me for a minute. My grandparents migrated from Scandinavia in the 1800s. They packed all their belongings into trunks that would be used in their new homes. The process that creates memories was beginning for them…and even for me. Imagine what it must have been like boarding a wooden ship that would sail across the Atlantic in who knows what kind of weather.

60

The goodbyes had been shared…stoic handshakes between the men and long hugs between the women. Remembering would be all that these families would have throughout the years ahead. These travelers would not be coming home to celebrate their birthdays. Celebrations and adventures in a new land…and remembering family back home.

Eventually, those passengers could maybe see a bit of land after many weeks on the ocean. Oh, the stories they must have shared with each other during those travel days. No cruise lines with mega-entertainment and glorious food at any time. And eventually, it would be the occasional letter back to family in Scandinavia telling more stories about their new home and asking about the welfare of family 'back home.'

I chose 'remembering' to begin my sharing with you. I am beginning my journey on paper rather than a wooden ship on the rough sea. I am, indeed, like those early travelers beginning a journey into the unknown of the future. I remember the process that seems to go round and round through endless generations, year after year. Read slowly and remember your journey. Read slowly and write down some of those unique, interesting, funny, unforgettable memories. Those who look back tomorrow will thank you for sharing your yesterdays.

REMEMBERING AN OLD STORY...

There was a man named Moses. The time surrounding his birth had been quite interesting. His life had been in danger, so his mother, seeking to protect him from certain death, made a waterproof basket and tucked Moses into his personal nest. The sister of Moses carried this precious cargo and placed it in the river near the bathing place of royalty.

Sure enough, the basket was sighted, not just by anyone. "Bring that basket to me," said the Queen (or maybe the Pharaoh's daughter), and they did just that, turning back the blanket to look at the startled face of this tiny being. His big sister jumped out of her hiding place and offered assistance with caring for this very young child. The Queen agreed, and a plan was made. Eventually, the palace playground would be most familiar to young Moses. I am guessing Moses had a lot of memories from those years.

Years went by as they do, and things changed for Moses. Moses saw some of the goings on in the royal workplace that didn't please him and, unwisely, took matters into his own hands. (But then, maybe that was a piece of the plan!) A wise decision prompted him to quickly move to a safer area. Moses settled in a new land, met his wife, and began a family. But then – much to his surprise – there was another change in the works.

(Isn't it interesting the similarity in our various journeys…Birth, life, and experiences in between those times.)

Moses was growing older. Sound familiar? He was caring for his family and living near his in-laws. What had been an ordinary life routine suddenly changed. Moses had an encounter with God!

As often happens in the lives of God's children, God had a plan for Moses. Moses had already been a busy husband and father for many years. His sons might have been grown by the time Moses had this conversation. His wife probably said, "You are going to do WHAT!" Moses might have replied, "God said my help was needed. The children of Israel are in trouble, and it seems that I am the one who needs to check this out."

Moses did not realize at this stage of the plan that God had something big in mind. You might know the feeling after having basically worked in your career, tended to your personal needs, and then…out of the blue! Who could have known!

Moses was on his way to see the Pharaoh. I don't even have a parallel experience to compare to what was ahead for Moses. Moses didn't know he was on the way to creating some pretty significant memories for generations ahead of him!

Moses arrived back in that familiar territory, and he was beginning to understand what God had in mind. About this time on the journey, Moses was probably wishing he was back home with his family. But God said, 'Moses, I need you to do something really big, really important." The plan was shared with Moses, and he said, "God, you must be kidding. I am growing too old for this kind of task. There must be someone else better suited. At least, isn't there someone who can do the talking for me if I do what you ask?"

Familiar words: *"Isn't there someone younger who can do this particular job?"*

Moses was probably remembering…thinking back on those years in the palace. Remembering the actions that got him into trouble. Remember how life had been for the Israelites. Moses surely remembered back on those years. Memories and fears. Moses knew God was not going to give up on this plan, and if Moses agreed to help, Moses knew God would not leave his side.

Whatever it was that caused Moses to willingly begin this journey…Moses began. Life is often like that. Just when we think all is in order, we are surprised as we either climb to the mountaintop or unexpectedly fall over a cliff. That is a bit dramatic, but basically, we begin with one step at a time, discovering one experience after another on this journey of aging. Moses wasn't working on a plan for AARP, but what we notice is that this journey began when Moses was already an older man. He meets with one challenge after another, and then, years later, God says, "Okay, Moses, your work has been completed. Good job done! The people you cared for are going to begin a new life in a new place, and you, Moses, are coming back up to the top of the mountain to be with me."

And as I share this story with you, you may notice that our stories are so similar. Life changes in ways we didn't expect. The experiences vary, but the memories that come together from our travels don't vary all that much.

Moses had retired. He hadn't planned on a second career. God had another plan. I have a friend who shared the story of her 'one-day' retirement. Laurel was certainly not as old as Moses, but she had just retired…that day. Laurel's daughter was a single mom with two young children, and after realizing that she needed to focus on a plan for her kids, this young mom decided to return to college. You know what comes next, don't you? Laurel's new job was multi-tasking – Grandma was caring for the little ones. Does that ring a bell with the job description for Moses? "Moses, I know you are growing older, but will you help guide my children as they are growing through so many changes?"

Moses and Laurel were both growing older. They were probably both remembering all they had accomplished in years past and might even have been thinking about some days of rest in the future. Both Moses and Laurel knew that God was going to be right there on the first day of work at their new job. Their lives changed. There was a new plan for them. I wonder if Moses and Laurel might have stopped for a minute on the way to work with the thought, "Do you remember when our kids were little, and we were busy with all that we had to do…." God's children and Laurel's grandchildren. Both back to providing 'child care' again.

A change appeared on their aging journey.

You will discover the Circle of Life looks familiar no matter who we are or what we do or where we live…or how old we are. Let sets remembering.

AS I CLOSE MY DAY ...

"I look up to the mountains. Does my strength come from the mountains?

No, my strength comes from God, who made heaven and earth, and mountains.

He won't let you stumble.

Your Guardian God won't fall asleep.

Not on your life!

Israel's Guardian will never doze or sleep.

God's your Guardian.

Right at your side to protect you –

Shielding you from sunstroke,

Sheltering you from moon stroke.

God guards you from every evil, he guards your very life.

He guards you when you leave and when you return.

He guards you now. He guards you always."

(Psalms 121)

(Eugene. H. Peterson crafted this from original languages in order to present its tone, rhythm, events, and ideas in everyday language.)

(THE MESSAGE - The Bible in Contemporary Language by EUGENE H. PETERSON Publication date/ 2002....ISBN 1-57683-289-9/ NAVPress)

I began this book with the short, sweet story of a little girl in the process of growing up to be a 'big girl.' That story was shared by a special friend. I am now adding a couple short aging stories by her husband. I smile when I am typing his words – he has so many good stories – but I think these will bring a smile to your face as well.

These last few years, I have become unnerved by certain phenomena unfolding in the world around us. In the first place, there is the increasing force of gravity. Small things such as a small table, for example, or a sewing machine in this case, which I used to be able to pick up with one hand, are now almost cemented to the floor by the power of gravity.

Just the other day, I was looking for a jar of mayonnaise in the refrigerator. I couldn't find it, so I asked my endlessly patient wife where it was. "Top shelf," she said. I looked at the top shelf. No sign. "I can't find it," I said. "It's right there, in front," she patiently responded. I looked again closely.

(The search goes on according to his story… and his wife finds the mayonnaise right where she said it would be)

Perry continues…In the wastes of the night, it (the jar of mayonnaise) probably gleefully reported its complete success of hiding in the refrigerator to the admiring herd of 'misplaced' eyeglasses who replied with their own individual triumphs, including the tortoiseshell pair retelling the classic trick of leaping atop my head just as I come into my wife's field of vision after complaining about having looked for my glasses all over the house! And there is the story of the glasses who managed to hide themselves right in the palm of my hand while I looked for them elsewhere.

We have been remembering all kinds of things that have made our lives what they are. When we remember, we are creating memories. Remembering comes from my own mind and personal experiences, but memories can be collected and shared. Memories can be pasted into a book or framed and hung on the wall. Our refrigerator door is a perfect place to put photo memories.

I find that it is important for me to sort through memories…those tangible memories. Organizing my 'remembering.' The more thought I put into this part of the aging process, the more ways I discover the best way of collecting all these things that are on my mind. My remembering storage plan…

I enjoy taking pictures whether it is on my phone or a 'real' camera. And I keep everything! We have been going through tons of photos with our daughter as she finds family history important at this stage in her life as well as ours. We are always wondering, "Do you know who that is? Do you remember where this was taken? "Do you remember?" comes up with almost every photo. Some because we have no idea about the image, and more often, one photo leads to many conversations.

And photos are just the beginning. We have plants and lamps on top of those old travel trunks from generations past. Now we must clean off the top and begin digging through. I do know my mother's wedding dress and hat are in one trunk. From all the earthly possessions of relatives beginning a new life in a new land to photo albums of our first house, vacations, or fun times with friends…there is much to organize. It's time to make choices of what we want or need to keep and what just must go in the dumpster. It's time to organize remembering and choose what memories are important to keep.

I purchased a lovely book that has pages with coverings so photos can be stored as well as pockets for odds and ends. It is all stable enough for those old heavy cardboard photos of my grandmother's era. As we sort through all of these memories, hopefully, those who look through these items will find it easier to understand the memory we so wisely chose to preserve. I have even made my own books where I write and collect memories. You can do the same with your memories.

Life on the farm had a much different flavor back then. There was a deep connection between the farmers and the work they had chosen for their life journey. Farming was hard work and to be a farmer, one had to love the work. I smile at the memories of my father, the farmer and his two best friends, both farmers.

These men were friends - buddies. Honest, hardworking and loved playing jokes on each other. Over the years I am sure they had their disagreements but they were friends. Friendship for them meant that they could support each other with needs that might come up as farmers. Friendship meant that they weren't in competition with each other. It was a time for these three farmers when life was more about the welfare of each other more than the rise to success they might experience as 'big farmers.

I grew up in an environment understanding the importance of loyalty and caring for your neighbor. The farmer who lived near our farm had a son my age. He, like me, watched his father go about his farming business with pride. But we also saw the world changing. The first change was that the children of these farmers didn't stay on the farm. They went to college to prepare for other means of employment. We left the farm and we didn't return to the farm.

Years later, John, the son of our neighbor decided to return to the farm and take up where his aging father had been showing signs of slowing down. Change continued. The cost of being a farmer soared. Buying machinery was an astronomical challenge. The weather was a challenge. Pests that attacked the crops were a challenge.

But with all these concerns, life on the farm was still good. John provided a good life for his family. Hunting, fishing, creating trails in the woods, being involved in their school activities were priorities for this farming family.

Change continued. John's children also left the farm. But unlike John, they didn't' return. Making a life for a family on the farm had become difficult for young families. Oh, the wonderful memories were still there. The grandchildren came to visit on the farm and do all those fun things their dad had done as a young boy. The picture was clear. Stepping into the role of an 'ordinary' farmer was becoming more and more difficult.

John and I both remember our mothers doing all the chores expected of a farmer's wife…also hard work. They worked at their homes, caring for the farmer who was busy caring for his farm.

Life was different. Life was changing. Farmers and their families were changing. The memories are still special but the places and events were changing. John and his wife still live on their farm. Their children still have created successful lives in other places. The farm is still in their hearts but the times have changed.

I feel as though our society has lost more than the small farm. Change is usually good and often inevitable. The world needs change to progress. But…there was something about life on the farm that has just become a memory.

I must tell you about my father. Of course, I didn't know him when he was a young man just beginning his personal life, but the photos tell quite a story about him. So many times, we have commented, "Did he really go fishing in the row boat wearing a suit and tie?" Yes, he did. "Was he that handsome a man…he could have been a model?" Yes, he most certainly was a good-looking gentleman, and he seemed to like to have his picture taken.

I don't know what he was thinking as a photo was taken, but I can imagine. Think about your parents before you were a part of their life responsibilities. The family members of my parent's generation are no longer living, so there is no one I can go to for answers to my questions. Now think about this…if I don't collect some of those memories, yet another generation will slip away from my heritage.

It isn't just my family memories…think about all the history that has been collected in libraries around the world. Tangible records. Dates, Certificates. How many people passed through Ellis Island. What is interesting is that many of those people simplified their names as they entered this new country. Names often described relationships, and as new ways developed, so did their names. The Son of Peter became Peterson. Makes sense to me.

Photos that show the environment of those days always get me thinking about what it must have been like to have no indoor plumbing, no electricity, no cars, and on and on. Eventually, indoor plumbing meant that there was a pump on the edge of the kitchen sink, a dry sink it was called, and that would bring small quantities of water actually into the house. Coal could be stored in the cellar so that wood did not need to be chopped and carried into the house in inclement weather. Kerosene lanterns provided light by which work could be done after dark. Probably safer than candles, but then again…

No, I don't want to return to pumping water, nor do I even want to consider a coal-burning stove in the center of the living area of my home. I don't want to go back to what seems to have been a lot of hard work. BUT…I do think about the simple life. Maybe that is why I think collecting those memories is important. I put life in perspective.

People worked hard generations ago…manual labor just to provide for each day. Some days when I am overwhelmed with my household tasks, I think… "Really? I am complaining about emptying the dishwasher. I am finding it hard to get to folding all that laundry! A snow-blower rather than shoveling through piles of drifting snow." Maybe the memories are important for other reasons than just remembering.

So my day begins…everything I need for breakfast is either in the refrigerator or my cupboards. I go to the closet and choose what to wear from far too many items on hangers. Some I haven't worn this season. If I am still going to work, the car is in the garage, and off I go on good roads. Maybe

I need to contact my husband during the day - my cell phone is in my pocket. It might be one of those evenings where a family schedule makes carry-out for dinner easier.

Are you getting the 'picture'? No, I don't want to go back to one item of clothing in the closet. I don't want to spend my morning collecting eggs from the henhouse or dressing to go to the barn to help with the morning milking. I don't want to do laundry in a washtub, hoping the clothes will dry in the cold outdoors. A kerosene lantern might make a room appear cozy, but I don't want that to be my light source after dark.

Collecting memories just might have an important purpose other than just for 'remembering.' Here I am…at an age where I need to be going through my earthly possessions. What am I going to do with all this stuff? Who wants the china…we already talked about that! And even living in a house that we chose, knowing that we are growing older…we have enough furniture for two families. I have 'extras' of too many things. What happened to living in 'simple fashion'? No, not moving back to the past but just living simply.

Our remembering will lead to so many memories. Memories that are precious, fun, important, and necessary, but think again about those memories. Can I learn something about who I am today, where it is that I am going in the future, and what it is I need…. Can I not only enjoy remembering but also learn from the memories?

My father mowed what seemed to be acres of the yard around our farmhouse. My mother seemed to spend the majority of her time cooking or baking. They enjoyed their neighbors who would stop by for coffee…unannounced! Can you imagine! They didn't travel far from their hometown. What they needed could be found in their own grocery or hardware store in their hometown down the road.

You are probably thinking…thank goodness times have changed. And I would agree, but it also causes me to stop and reflect on my lifestyle. Do I need three sets of dishes? You know, the everyday dishes in the kitchen cupboard and the fancy China maybe is set for dinner only on holidays which is when we quietly complain of needing to wash them by hand. And then something just a bit nicer than every day just in case someone 'drops by.' Who needs all those dishes? Without even thinking, I wear a shirt one time and then toss it in the dirty clothes basket.

Do I need to do laundry so often? Our hometown is larger than the town where I grew up, but it is interesting that the things we sometimes 'need' are an hour away in the 'big city.'

Maybe the remembering and the memories are leading me in a direction for some life changes. Don't tell me that growing older means I can't change…or don't need to change. Recycling can be a nuisance, but… Using paper instead of plastic might not be convenient, but…. Throwaway sure can make clean-up easier, but…

I think that it is important to remember the memories and what it is that I am going to do with all the material goods that fill my life. I think that talking with our daughter about how we did laundry years ago should trigger a thought in my mind about how it is that I casually toss clothes in the washer today. I am thinking that when I tell our grandson how good homemade bread is compared to 'store bread,' maybe I could try baking bread once in a while. Do I need to drive into town for just one thing I forgot to pick up at the grocery?

Ah, remembering is going to challenge me to consider some life changes, even at my age. What if our grandson told his friends, "My granny makes the best bread!" and his friends asked, "How does she do that?" I don't need batteries to read a good book or put together a puzzle on a quiet evening. And a quiet evening is good. I don't need to have a full calendar each day.

Are you getting the picture? We can change – even at our age. We can at least give it a try. I don't want to get in trouble explaining my thoughts about memories, but I do think it is worth considering. Re-tire doesn't mean that I am getting tired all over again. These are the quiet days of my life, and I want to choose wisely.

I am growing older, and life is most certainly different from the days when I was living in a farmhouse in Minnesota. And that was all good for those times. Times have changed, but in recognizing that fact, I also need to ponder the memories I am sorting through as I sit quietly, thinking about these questions that can bring changes in my life.

Give it some thought.

MORE OF MY STORY…

Interesting how all this aging thing is playing out on paper. I began to think about beginnings and in doing so I started remembering so many things. The remembering led to actually looking around in my house, wondering what I should be putting away or what memories of a more tangible nature should be kept. Changes so often affect the memories what we tend to remember and what we would rather forget.

There have been significant changes in my life. One I distinctly remember began during the first months of being a college student. I had no idea about what a life path might look like. What I wanted to do with my life had never really required much planning for the future time. Off to college, I went…future unknown.

The first semester passed by, but my grades left something to be desired. Those courses just were not my cup of tea. I had been considering a career in some kind of social work because that is what women did, I thought. I spent that first summer at summer school, catching up. I thought I was going to play piano with a group at a summer resort…change of plans!

The second year arrived and I was not much wiser. You would think that I would have learned something. I did learn something that I didn't realize I was learning. I was excited to see that an elective was available in my schedule as class planning began. Hm, an art class, drawing to be specific. I had no art experience and had never been to a real art museum. Should I or shouldn't I? I did. A drawing class and it was entirely amazing! Now that was something that most certainly managed to fill my soul. I was where I was supposed to be. I was about to become an art student!

The world opened for me. Probably not much different than coming to America from a country far away. Was my enthusiasm any less (different maybe) than those travelers? I was finding my way and my heart was full. My ancestors didn't become well-known pioneers and I didn't become a well-known artist but we were finding our path to what it was that mattered in our lives.

These, both for me and for my ancestors, were significant life changes. How often do I just go along, taking one step at a time, not thinking about where those steps are taking me? How often do I simply accept what I think isn't going to change in life, paying no attention to those feathers that fall from the sky? How often am I just simply unwilling to consider change?

Change happens. Of course, there are going to be tangled roots on the path and of course, I just might stumble or lose our way but that's change! Maybe I didn't fear change as much when I was younger. Change at my age can mean as much in my life now as it meant to those young immigrants arriving in America! I'm not going to wait to see what tomorrow brings when I am presented with some changes on my path. I can do this!

ANOTHER OLD STORY…

Moses and God are still wondering how they are going to get all those people out of Egypt. The Pharaoh was quite the opposite. Frogs, bugs - nothing seemed to cause him to change his mind about letting these people go. Change was not on the mind of the Pharaoh!

Moses and God got their plan together. This was going to be a monumental change for the Israelites. Life in Egypt wasn't good, but what Moses was suggesting – well, they thought they would give it a try. This change put everything in the hands of God and Moses. The people were leaving everything behind, going where they had not been, and having no idea of what was going to happen when they arrived. God had made a promise to take care of them, but this was more than what they had expected.

Over and over, Moses reminded them that, even though this was a huge change for them, God wouldn't let them be out there in the wilderness on their own. Cloud in the day and fire at night – God wouldn't leave them.

But those Israelites were much like me when it came to change. They forgot what had been their life and behaved like children…angry, pouting, and wanting it their way when the walk took longer than they expected. Remember that reference to being angry at the snow…well, being angry with God's plan was kind of like being angry at the snow. As much as they complained, the plan was going to be before them. Only their willingness to manage and accept the change God was putting before them was going to make this trip what God intended.

I would rather tell you that all went well, and they were quickly at their destination, but that was not the case. Traveling lasted so long that it was the next generation who stepped into this new plan that God and Moses had shared with them for so long.

Moses reminded them over and over again, "You and I and God can do this. I know the change is more than you bargained for, but if we work together, we can do this!" The original travelers just couldn't get it through their stubborn minds...Don't tell me what to do! Whose idea was this in the first place?

The story continues in Exodus, where you can read about these complaining people. The story is interesting, and I think God is leading us to learn about how we behave on our life journey. Often, we travel our journey, and there needs to be changes. AAA made an error, and that road just wasn't on the map! Or maybe I read the map incorrectly! Changes happen, and sometimes that brings some significant baggage with it...fear, anger, confusion, and frustration. We become nervous about not seeing what is ahead. Kind of like being in the middle of the Atlantic on that wooden ship, wondering just where this New Land might be. Let me remind you...and me...that being angry during change is not going to cause the change to disappear! We will think more about that in just a bit.

LORD,

I never did think much about change. I just put my clothes in the closet at night and before I know it, another day begins. Everything seems to be just as I left them last night.

LORD,

Change seems to disrupt all that has been comfortable…at least what I thought was 'comfortable'. Life seemed to be going along just fine and then this getting older, for instance, is dumped on me. Did that have to be a part of your plan?

LORD,

You said you would take me 'just as I am' and right now I am not too pleased about what is happening to my body. I wake up stiff and go to bed tired after not doing all that much. Aches and pains…getting older is hard work.

LORD,

If you could help me understand that change is what is going to be the 'new normal' in this aging body, I would appreciate it. Change is a challenge but I am willing to work with you! I guess acceptance is an important piece in this part of my life.

LORD,

I will give these changes a try (what else can I do) but I am not promising to do so without a bit of complaining. Thank you for traveling with me – just as I am!

SOMETHING FOR YOU TO DO…

I might have mentioned this previously, but I tend to learn/understand a situation better if I can sit quietly and write about what I am processing. These changes don't happen all at once, and once one change is conquered, don't think there is not another crook on the road again. I don't mean to scare you, but that is just how change works.

So, it's time for you to think about change in your life and just how it is that you are managing change. I smile to myself when I think you might need more space to write about change than what is provided here in this book!

What has it been for you? Retirement isn't what you expected. The empty nest was tougher than you thought it would be. You must be kidding…sell my house!

Start the list. Be honest. Try not to approach this with fear in your heart. It's just change. Looking at change, straight on is far healthier than thinking it is the monster under the bed. What you do with the list is up to you. It might even lead you to consider adopting more comfortably…and wisely. Just don't ignore facing the changes that are going to be on your path.

It seems that I am a bit down on change. Not so. I recognize the possibilities of change, but I am also very open to the enthusiasm that change might present in my day. Something new. Something different. Something to challenge me during an ordinary day. Change just might be a feather on your path, and as I have said before…you can do this – whatever the change might be.

A page for your thoughts

FORGETTING IS SO FRUSTRATING…

It has been years and years since my first teaching position. My high school art students were good farm kids who seemed open and excited about the motivational ideas I planned for their creative exploring. One of the popular songs during this time was entitled "Turn, Turn, Turn" (Not difficult to remember those words!) The words were meaningful to me and seemed to open all kinds of potential for creating. "There is a time for everything" and 'everything' described a variety of thoughts in the course of the song. There is a time for everything under the sun. Think about that.

There are some things in my life that I hadn't considered…hadn't thought that there would be a time when I would worry about being forgetful, for instance. Another piece of the circle of life…forgetting. I was going to change the word 'worry' to assure you that I wasn't worried, but that wouldn't be the truth.

Yes, I do worry when I forget those ridiculously simple things. I don't know if this should come before the challenges of 'change' or just where it fits, but I know for sure that forgetting is real for all of us during our journey with aging.

Again, don't let this be the ghost in the closet! We are in this together. If I meet you on the street and don't remember your name, that's okay. We can still enjoy a conversation before we are on our way again. What I am saying is that 'forgetting' is so familiar to most of us 'seniors!

Our grandson is an avid reader. He carries books home from the library by the bagsful. This particular school year, his class participates in Battle of the Books. The students are given a long list of books to read, and at the end of the school year, there is a 'battle' related to what they remember from their reading. We talked about the process one day, and I asked him how he could remember all of that information. (Name of author and name of the book where the incident is related to the story.) "How do you remember all those authors, books, stories, and characters?" I was overwhelmed by the thought. I was even more overwhelmed when he didn't seem concerned about remembering so much!

But…I am a bit older, and maybe, when I was the age our grandson is now, I could have remembered a bit of that as well. When I was growing up, the world of technology, as I now experience it, was unheard of. I didn't need to know my house number, and my telephone number was simply…3L. A free calendar from the local grain elevator (their advertising) was where we recorded dates that needed to be remembered. Television provided three stations, and one of those stations was in French from Canada! The daily news could easily slip by unless it happened on our front doorstep. There were far more things we didn't have as compared to what we now have! Could it be that there wasn't as much to remember?

I don't have research to back up this example, but I have a feeling that my brain is overloaded. I am especially speaking as an older adult…I can't keep up! My mind is full to the point of overflowing. Young people are embarking on careers that I can't even spell. They travel internationally. I recently flew to Minnesota by myself. I knew just what I had to do, where to go to do it, and then…I just did it. I repeatedly checked my watch so that I wouldn't forget what time passengers were on board the plane. I dug through my purse frequently to be sure I had the keys to the rental car. I like a paper ticket because I can hold it in my hand rather than aimlessly search for the necessary information on my phone. An assortment of concerns, but each one was directly related to the fear I would forget to do something and would be left standing in an empty airport after every other person had remembered what to do and when to do it. Exaggeration…yes, but again you can relate to the importance of the concept of 'forgetting.'

And then there are all the 'toys' for kids that I can't figure out how to play. It is the pages of directions that throw me for a loop! What was the next step? Do I move … how many spaces, and then I do what? It was much easier to play 'Sorry' or even the early addition of 'You Remember the Game' – "Do not pass go. Do not collect $200. Yes, that's the one."

If you are old enough to have had a Medicare annual physical, you will identify with this and smile.

Remember the Medicare 'senior questions?

It is about following directions, repeating directions, remembering directions…and that deadly one that you will most certainly recall. The nurse asks all the correct questions about medications, health, and if you still live at the same address. Then, she says, "Please remember these three words!" Yikes! This is the part where I wish I had written those words on the back of my hand!

Her questions continue, and then all of a sudden comes the surprise question, "Do you remember the three words I gave you earlier?" *No*! No, I don't. Maybe one of the words was…oh, I don't remember them. It happens every year. Everything else goes wonderfully well but just because I can't remember those three ridiculous words. Oh no…I failed the Medicare test! NO! I don't remember them, thank you!

Why am I so defensive about 'forgetting'? Was it easier to write a previous chapter about remembering…Or have I already written about this and forgotten? It's not going to be a good day!

I grew up on a farm – remember? As the years passed, my brain seemed to be like the big rain tub that stood near the garden. A gentle rain would slowly add to the water level, but when there was a heavy rainstorm, the tub overflowed. My aging brain reminds me of the overflowing tub. I have so many passwords written in a little black book, cell phone contact numbers on my phone, and a calendar that magically is updated when something new is happening in my life. I don't even have to make the entry, but I usually forget where to find the calendar on my phone! Forgetting just seems to add a whole different dimension to my idea of growing older. The rainwater is running over the sides of the tub!

Okay, so you are getting the picture of my brain overload that is often filed under 'I Forget!"

Do I need to research to confirm that there are a lot of things that I have the potential to forget simply because there are just too many things to remember? Google Search has become my go-to place when I am wondering about what I am forgetting…I am now considering another piece to that circle of life that is, for me, a bit more frightening. No, I mean a lot more frightening. When I was writing about remembering, I intended to think back on all those memories and all the interesting events that happened in my younger years. *Forgetting* is a whole new ballgame. Forgetting means that I just simply don't remember.

<u>Another funny story.</u>

My husband was not feeling well. I was out and about, and he asked that I bring home something vanilla or something other from McDonalds …something cold and easy to eat. I was in the drive-through line, then ordered, then paid, and then drove off and went home. When I arrived home, it hit me. I did all the things to complete the task, BUT I forgot to complete the task. I forgot to pick up the order! I was embarrassed. I was upset with myself. I even used some language I will not include here! Why was this simple moment so significant? It wasn't serious – I just forgot!

Do you know why…I think forgetting is frightening. There are too many 'what-ifs' when one considers forgetting. I don't want to go there, but for some reason, my brain is in charge of that one! Even as a child, we were put on the spot just because we forgot something. Mom asks as you leave for school, "Don't forget your lunch!" (Note the negative approach to the question.) Or maybe it is the question the teacher asks when you can't find your library book on library day. "You can't take out a new book if you 'forgot' your book from last week!" I forgot all those terms for my biology test, forgot to bring in the mail, forgot to pay a bill, forgot my cousin's birthday… Come on, these are no big deal! But they are because I experience forgetting in such a negative way. I forgot!

You are right – as younger people, we don't even think about the event when we forget something. Do it over and move on. I am no longer young, and when I forget something, I look upon the incident as the collapse of the world order. I agree; this is something that happens as we grow older. For instance, I am with friends, and we are remembering something we had all done together. We shared all the details and laughed at what had happened. I am quiet during the conversation. I am trying to recall this most humorous incident that everyone else has remembered. Then someone says directly to me, "You don't remember that? How could you forget?" But I did…I forgot what everyone else remembered. I didn't remember the event, but I sure remembered how I felt when I 'forgot'!

Yes, this happens more frequently as we grow older. Yes, I do remember that I commented on the fact that just becoming angry does nothing to prevent forgetting. It just might be that this chapter is going to be longer because forgetting seems to be more frustrating than other pieces of aging. Where did I put my phone? Or my keys? Did I share the story of Perry searching everywhere for his glasses just to find them in his hand? How on earth does one forget where one's glasses are when they are in their hand? Never fear, my friend…I know just how that could happen!

Stop. Take a breath. It is important to add a thought about forgetting. I am not referring to a serious medical condition related to dementia. I am not a medical professional, nor am I sharing that journey with someone dear to me. I am an ordinary aging person visiting with you, another ordinary aging person. Don't read my book when' forgetting' becomes a critical concern. That is the time to seek medical information with someone who most certainly knows more about that than the stories I am sharing with you.

TAKE A MINUTE TO SIT QUIETLY;

There are so many stories in the Bible where God's children have gotten into some kind of situation where they are frustrated or afraid because of what was happening to them. Often, they had forgotten the plans that God had shared with them.

Maybe God's children weren't forgetting their keys or wondering where they left their glasses. It wasn't what they were forgetting or why they were forgetting…it was just that they 'forgot.' Because of what they forgot or weren't aware of, they found themselves feeling afraid.

Afraid. Fearful. I forget why I walked into the room. I forgot an appointment that I didn't write on the calendar. I forgot to put that check in the mail to pay the electric bill. It's not that the things I forgot were such monumental experiences. I can always reschedule an appointment.

No, that's not it.

Forgetting, as I age, causes me to wonder and worry and feel concerned simply because I don't remember. To be completely honest, I find it more than a little scary. What if I forget something really important? Well, that adds fuel to the fire, and I worry some more. Worry does me no good! Worrying just leads me to feel fearful about my worrying. Kind of like a hamster running around on its wheel!

Even when the calendar years stack up…and maybe especially then…God puts a loving arm around us when we feel afraid. Not the kind of afraid that we used to experience when we were little and afraid of the dark but the kind of fear that we experience because we are growing older. It's not just the car keys…it's about 'forgetting.' I become fearful of the unknown, and being forgetful is just one more reminder of my aging journey.

For various reasons and in a variety of situations through the Bible, God has comforted people who were surrounded by fear. God has something to say regarding these feelings. God says, 'Don't be afraid! Over and over again, these words are given to us to calm our worries so that fear doesn't fill our hearts and souls. I know well-meaning friends might say, "Don't worry. It will be okay." That is not what God is saying. This is my Creator, who knew me before I saw the light of the day. This Creator is speaking and telling you and me…. "**Don't be afraid.** I've got this!"

Yes, I am going to forget where things are. I am going to forget to do certain things. I might forget someone's name…but it isn't the things that happen…it is the experience of forgetting and being afraid because I am growing older…

And God says to each one of us in whatever situation that causes us to feel fear, "**Don't be afraid.**" That is one thing not to forget! I believe God understands aging worry thinking about the unknown, and being afraid. When God says to me on this journey of growing older, **"Don't be afraid.** You aren't on this journey alone!"

Well, that's my Creator speaking…the one who planned my journey from the beginning.

God, if you keep your strong and loving arms around me, I know I can do this. Stop. Take a breath, and don't forget this promise.

SOMETHING FOR YOU TO DO...

I could continue with endless stories, some would bring a chuckle, and many would sound like you have walked in my shoes. I am not going to continue with more reminders of what I am forgetting, and instead, let's have some fun with not forgetting!

In so many instances where we experience challenges, there are 'things' we can do to help relieve the frustrations of what is challenging us. I tend to write. I take notes for just about anything. That is not because I am into a great research plan, but I tend to forget if I don't write down what it is that I want to remember. I was with a group of friends at a Bible study, but I wasn't contributing much verbally. At the next session, the leader commented that he was 'waiting to hear from me.' I assured him that I was involved but that it was so helpful to keep my pen and the thoughts of the group connected. I 'remember' through my writing.

Are there ways that techniques work for you when you think, "I don't want to forget to…" Some of those important 'remembering to do' things, such as taking my medicine on time, are important, not just humorous stories. All of a sudden, it is noon, and I think, "I forgot to take my medicine!"

My husband and I each have our part of the financial tasks in our family. I deal with the day-to-day issues like being sure there are no bills under all the stuff on my desk, bills I might have forgotten to pay. Yes, remembering to be diligent with responsibilities is an important day-to-day issue for me. Maybe I should include a chapter on organization!

Appointments are not meant to be forgotten. I make an appointment so that I can be where I need to be to do what it is that needs to be done. An appointment that has been made keeps the life of the person I am going to see organized and manageable. If I don't take note of that certain time for an appointment, I am not just confusing my day, but I am sharing that confusion with others.

Agreed…some facets of forgetting can be managed. So let's think about that…There are some things that I can do so that forgetting doesn't cause me to feel so 'frustrated (and dare I say it, angry!)

Another space for you to do some thinking. Consider just this one day. Is there something that you simply need to remember? What seems to work best for you…a calendar on your phone, a paper calendar, a post-it on your refrigerator? Become aware of how you remember or why you seem to forget. It might even be helpful to share the process with someone who is familiar with your daily life. Again, I am not referring to serious medical conditions. I am sharing our ordinary aging experiences.

Okay, what about those long-term events all of a sudden are right in front of you? Give your 'forgetting' a fun kick in the butt. There are so many crazy calendars…some have jokes, and others have daily cartoons. Some have a 'get you going' quote – make a fun calendar a daily go-to. Many such calendars have smaller daily pages that can easily be taken off each day. When one, in particular, touches your funny bone or is meaningful on a special day…post it somewhere special. You could start an 'Anti-Forgetting' wall or journal, adding all those reminders that made our aging journal an adventure.

And one last thought…I am not the only older person for might forget a thing or two. If you have a good idea about what helps you with this concern, share it with others. Post a little story on FB if you use such a social conversation. Tell a friend how something worked for you when he/she is sharing an incident of forgetting.

We can do this. Hopefully, we will grow older for a long while, so keep up with the plans to clear your path of all the unnecessary clutter along the way. Happy traveling.

Oh, one more thought. Don't be too hard on yourself when you forget. Just do something to make remembering easier. Don't tell yourself that no one else forgets their phone, keys, or glasses…they do! Don't think that everyone else is organized…they aren't! Don't allow anger to creep in, thinking that no one else gets upset when they forget…they do!

We are going to make the best of a most frustrating experience.

We can do this!

Patient Creator

I don't know if this is a prayer or just a conversation, but then, I guess they are one and the same.

I forgot to make time to talk with you yesterday. There were so many things on my mind. Nothing significant, but I just got busy. Maybe it is because I am growing older, but sometimes I forget the important things – like talking with you.

I'm busy today as well, but I just wanted to spend a minute letting you know that I am doing well. I had an important phone call, and yes, I took notes rather than thinking that I would just remember all that information.

I have an appointment this afternoon and a couple other things that need to be done – and yes, I have marked them on the calendar.

I'm also going to remember one additional important fact of life…I am not the only one who forgets. Remind me of that, Lord, when I forget that I am not growing older alone.

Lord,

Thanks for the reminders.

ANOTHER OLD STORY…

This old story will be short and rather general compared to the specific things in which Moses has been involved. There are a plethora of stories related to our individual faith journeys. The stories began so very long ago. I smile when I read about any task God had in mind, and the writer refers to a thought such as "God was thinking about…." I don't know what God is thinking, but I do know that God is on the job in a way that only God could be.

I do know for sure that we, God's family, have had opportunities for a lot of guidance over one generation after another. Adam forgot that God had already told him about that off-limits tree in the garden. Abram thought more about himself than how Sarai felt when he told her to tell the Pharaoh that she was really Abram's sister, not his wife. The Israelites forgot about how difficult life was in Egypt as they complained during their walk to freedom. King Saul seems to have forgotten that he had looked upon David as a son, and now he was throwing spears at him.

So many wonderful old stories with life examples to which I can relate. The stories might be old, but the experiences continue to live within us. Those folks were ordinary people, growing older and forgetting things that were important. I have used the comment from God in other places, but here it is once more…I get upset when I forget the simplest of things. I experience a variety of emotions when I forget important things. And what does God tell me, "Don't be afraid. I've got this."

It is one old story after another, but don't be afraid, my friends. We are walking together and supporting each other on our journey. Don't be afraid.

Lord, remind me to make time for you…each day.

"Just when the caterpillar thought the world was over, it became a butterfly."

Some techniques with my artwork can become quite a process, one step after another with some pauses in between to ponder the process. A few months ago, I was invited to speak to a group and was given a topic on which to focus my presentation. Interesting topic, I thought. Process! Being an artist, I was certainly familiar with the concept of process, but as for speaking about process…what would I say to this group that would be interesting to them?

Well, if a caterpillar could figure it out, certainly, I could do so also. My career in the arts had come somewhat as a surprise. Realizing that I was probably not going to maintain a lifestyle or put groceries in the cupboard selling my artwork, I chose to become a visual arts teacher, eventually working with students of all ages and abilities. I learned many techniques rather than just focusing on one area. The more years I taught, the more proficient I became in a variety of techniques.

As I stepped into retirement years, I had more time to concentrate on my own personal work. I began the process by actually living and working with the idea of the process. Recently, one evening I shared a video with our grandson that was made when he was just a little guy. He was 'creating' and was very confident with his work. As he was working, he was quietly singing…something he continues to do when he is pleasantly involved with whatever the process. As I was following him with my camera, I said, "You are a wonderful artist!" to which he responded, "I know!" Complete confidence in what he was doing. Yesterday we sat together in the sunroom, each at different stage of our lives, and once again, we were creating. Both of us are on our individual journeys, exploring our own processes.

This morning I was reviewing photos of flowers which I had taken. My purpose had been to focus on the unique aspect of each flower, whatever it's stage of growth. So many things contributed to its uniqueness – size, stage of growth, color, and shape to list just a few. Many flowers were various kinds of orange, running the gamut from very light to dark. Some flowers produced a sweet scent, and others not so much, but generally, there seemed to be some kind of scent that would draw the attention of a creature that would feed off the plant. And…some of the blooms were bending down to the ground, dropping their seeds back into the earth to once again, at a later time in the seasons, to once again begin the cycle. We aren't always aware of the process, but often, we find ourselves commenting, "There are more wildflowers this spring," or maybe, "I wonder why the iris is blooming so wonderfully this season?" We are probably more aware of a particular aspect of the plant/flower but don't pay as much attention to the process.

So, I was thinking about what I would say to this group. What did I want to share about the process? Process…an activity. So, in the beginning, I organized what it was that I would need to get started. Some beginnings provide their own 'supplies.' Other beginnings are something that I can actually plan. Then there is the time for planning…what will I create? What do I want to do with my life? This period of time most certainly will vary for each one of us. Then comes the work…will my creation be messy so that I need to prepare the area where I am working. Will the work of my life move forward smoothly? I figure most of us have some ups and downs. Who knows when the process will be completed? As for my artwork, I can kind of determine how long the process will take. With my life journey, I can't be too sure.

My 'process' ideas were coming together for my presentation.

I have memories tucked away that go back as far as I can remember. As kids, we long to 'be older,' but the aging process tends to find its own pace. We begin as a babe in arms, becoming an 'into everything' toddler, an 'excited to be growing up' teenager, and before we know it, we are considering what it is that will make up our personal life journey as we move forward. Years pass with one experience after another.

Each year has an agenda with reminders noted on the calendar. Each year seems to be filled with responsibilities and requirements. Find a job, tend to your finances, clean your house and do the laundry, remember the birthdays of family members, be kind, help others, and the list continues depending on your journey. There are challenges, and there are joys. There are health concerns, and there are fun adventures. During all these years, this period of time seems to be the 'meat of the life process.

Then one year, one month, one day brings that astonished look on my face, and I think, "FIFTY!" Surely this isn't happening already! I continue to be surprised with a birthday as each decade arrives. *Sixty…seventy*…Are there still more? What is interesting is that I continued to be surprised that I am growing older and that the speed with which I do so seems to have increased. Okay, eighty…I am going to celebrate when that day comes. No more of this 'shocked to be older' stuff.

Aging needs some humorous stories…we were new to a community and had been invited to a surprise birthday for an older gentleman. Not knowing the specifics of the party, I talked with a neighbor whom I knew had also been invited. When I shared my concerns, my neighbor smiled, "For many years, his wife has surprised him with a 'surprise' birthday party!" That sort of took the edge off the surprise part of the event. Maybe more and more birthdays take us by surprise more than I realize.

I am going to share a bit with you, and this part becomes more difficult. I will move forward gradually as this part of life requires my full attention. I think back over all these past decades. I have actually experienced all the things about which I have written. As I mentioned, there have been ups and downs. There were those many months when I felt robbed of time during my cancer journey. I have grown during the years of retirement. We have had such exciting times on various vacations. There are still so many blessings we share with family, being so grateful to be a part of their younger lives. Retirement also brought the blessings of new friends as we moved to a new 'growing older' home. Oh, this has been a long process…this living my life.

My life process is presenting new challenges and changes, some exciting and others a bit more challenging. I continually learn more and more about acceptance. As the work comes to a close, I think back on my art history studies, where I learned about the architects of the magnificent cathedrals from centuries ago. As the builders completed their work on an arch, for instance, there was one last piece. It is called a capstone or keystone. Almost magically, this piece would be dropped into the final space as the two sides of the arch come together. Bingo! The arch goes on to be strong and firm for centuries. All has been completed.

Oh, I don't mean to make it all that simple, but you get the idea. This piece is important…and necessary. Our daughter knew that I had been focused on writing about aging, and she recently shared a wonderful podcast with me. The conversation between the two commentators began quite casually until one of them shared an experience that involved her young daughter. And the conversation grew in intensity…it led into thoughts about the end of life. Notice that I didn't use the word 'death.' We call death by so many less offensive words. Anything but that ghost in the closet or the monster under the bed terms. Never the word that makes the end of life so final. Our culture tends to become quite creative with just what we call this last capstone as we put in place the last piece in the circle of life.

Death is real, but death also burrows so deeply into the innermost place in our hearts and soul. It brings with it emotions of loss and sadness even before it actually happens. It causes grief and tears and anger as that final piece is put into place.

And then…you know where I am going with this…

Death may be the final piece to the circle of life, but the experience might cause that capstone in our 'real life' situation to require some adjusting. I'm not talking about the old cathedral now…I am talking about what we all will face on our life journey.

It doesn't seem to matter if the death is expected or that it knocked me off my feet with the blow. It might seem to take the very breath from my lungs. It might have seemed to be 'appropriate' and timely, maybe because death didn't arrive until many years into the life a person had lived. On the other hand, unexpected death has the potential to cause anger stronger than we could have imagined possible. That kind of death leaves feelings of a life 'unfinished,' and we just can't imagine how that could have happened. Sometimes death seems to take forever, and other times, in the blink of an eye, it happens. It is always so difficult to let go.

As you read through this chapter, you might be thinking, "I don't want to read one more word of this 'end of life' business. I don't want to think about it!" Capstone…could it be that I am afraid that if I thought about my circle of life ending, I just might be overwhelmed by the thought of the circle closing? Being completed. I have so many plans still on my plate. I might not just be dealing with a word I don't like, but I might be facing some feelings I don't like – or that I don't know how to process. Ah, that 'process' word again, and it is still an action verb in so many ways. How am I going to move through those days of loss and sadness, confusion and grief?

There isn't a one size fits all capstone in life. The definition of the capstone isn't going to settle in one's heart the same for all of us. The end of life will be a different process for each person. Death is going to be there, and we must learn to talk about it. Death is not just a 'done deal,' and we easily move on. It just doesn't happen that way.

I would like to write another chapter where I could provide specific directions for how to manage death at an older age. I don't know how to do that. I could probably use one more chapter for an unexpected death, but I don't know how to do that either. There are endless chapters that could be written to make death easier, but they wouldn't make the actual 'process' any easier. The chapters have the potential to go on and on, but I simply can't give you any packaged directions. There must be hundreds of books dealing with death. I think those books provide valuable information, studies of what seems to be helpful, suggesting ways in which to move forward, and describing how our emotions affect life… these books and information can be very helpful.

BUT…my actual experience with death is unique to who I am as an individual. My fears might process differently than another person's. My tears might flow more furiously than those of another individual. My anger might seem out of control to others. Someone may question my acceptance. Or vice versa.

I could share stories about the aging process because we can chuckle at similar experiences. I can provide you some step-by-step ideas that might work for ghost removal…BUT no, I can't give you specific directions for experiencing death. That might sound harsh, but it's reality. I don't have a user manual for dealing with death.

BUT…I do have something else to offer. Love, support, hugs, and time to share when life seems empty. During this time that will seem to shake your very foundation, God stands by a Promise. Actually, it is kind of a double-duty promise. It is a gift for us as we participate in the process of the death of someone dear to us…those of us who remain in this life. It is also a gift for the one who has completed the circle of life, their own journey of aging. Yes, it has both a warranty and a guarantee. It is a promise that is valid at any time or place, or circumstance. It is one of those 'for sure' kinds of promises.

I think of death as similar to the thought I shared about remembering memories. Two pieces in the circle. One piece provides me with opportunities to look back on what was to what had been. I can quietly remember in my mind or maybe even share stories as we have done together on these pages.

As in remembering and keeping tangible memories, the other part of death is something that requires involvement, one day at a time. We learn, explore, and try new things. One step forward, another back…and gradually, it will be two steps forward. This piece of recovering after death is unique as well. The loss has been real. The pain and the tears are real. Feeling lost and alone are real. BUT…there is that word again…but when my heart gradually settles down, there is a space that opens to the love others have to offer. And gradually, another opening appears, and one slowly responds to the hugs and support, and love that others have to share. This is not a solo performance…I don't do this alone.

Life is interesting. A new baby enters the world, and one's heart is so filled with emotion. Sometimes tears are the only way to express these deep feelings. And then, whenever it might happen, the experience of death once again causes my heart to work overtime. I can't find the words, so the tears take over.

Oh, my caterpillar friend…I understand what certainly seemed to be over. Done, finished, completed. But then it became a Butterfly. When your heart feels empty, remember the butterfly. It's not over.

LORD,

Endings can be so difficult. For some things in my life, it is natural to see an event completed even though I don't want that vacation to end or a really good book finally reach the last chapter. But that is just a vacation or a book.

LORD,

Some endings seem so 'forever.' That's where I get stuck. Help me remember that what seems to be forever to me doesn't mean that I am going to have to deal with this alone. I might keep the door to my heart closed too long, but deep down, I know you have the key, and you will not forget that I need your company. You don't even need to knock.

LORD,

When my heart is empty and so focused on loss – okay, I will say the word – focused on death, hold my hand, and keep me close. One day at a time.

LORD,

For a while, I have more tears to shed than words to write. I know that you are close by. We can talk more soon.

I NEED THEM BOTH – PHYSICAL AND INNER STRENGTH

How can I find the strength to do something when I no longer seem to be strong? At this point in my life, I am pleased to report that I can manage that impossible cover on the milk cartons, and I can still win in art wrestling with our grandson! Grandmas might not be the whiz they would like to be on computer games, but for now, this grandma has a pretty good arm. That cover on some grocery items – who do they think is going to try to break into a milk carton!

I am reasonably healthy and physically sound but don't get up from the floor well. I laugh and tell my husband that I look like a giraffe trying to get up out of a shoebox! I don't kneel at communion and appreciate help carrying the groceries in from the car. As I become older, I understand things such as strength with a new approach. Physical strength isn't about arm wrestling when I am almost eighty years old. I am really considering the strength that comes from within, which keeps me on task and helps me remain motivated when I seem to lose interest. Physically, I am no longer as strong as I used to be…but let's think about another kind of strength.

I'm older now. I don't mind asking for help with the milk container, and I think a bit more about my inner strength. Not being able to lift that heavy box from the floor doesn't need to upset me. Inner strength isn't bothered by lifting or moving things. Being fearful and thinking about what I can or can't do is another of those yin-yang things. When I concentrate on all those amazing feats I used to be able to accomplish, getting upset because I can no longer do some of those things now…remembering that pushes me into competition with **fear**. Knowing what I cannot do quickly gives fear the outside edge. Fear is the cousin of 'can't and they would both love to arm wrestle me right to the ground. Fear keeps whispering in my ear that 'older' people can't do 'that' whatever 'that' might be. Fear wants nothing more than to push inner strength right out the door.

Have I mentioned stubbornness yet? It's another family member of fear. Growing up in northern Minnesota, where there are no hills, didn't provide an opportunity for me to learn how to downhill ski. For a period of time, a student from England, a young man not much older than our daughter, became a part of our family. He was an avid skier and had skied in the Alps! I was impressed.

Remember that these kids are young…me, not so.

For Christmas, one of the years he was with us, I gifted our family, as a surprise, with a ski trip. And here comes the story of overcoming fear with stubbornness. Everyone was having a good time skiing down the 'real' slopes while I was messing around on the bunny slopes. Eventually, it was time to go home, and I was yet to have fun! To the lift I went, ski gear ready, and found myself on the way to a blue slope. Guess who I met as I got off the lift. My kids! "What are you doing here? How do you plan to get down safely?"

Not to worry. I would come up with a plan. "I am going to ski down," I said without hesitating. And without much more conversation, I turned, pointed my skis downhill, and away I went. I passed everyone on the way down, but I remained upright. Then I became aware that now I had better come up with a plan for stopping at the bottom. I could do it. Who were they to determine what I could or could not do! I just sat down on my skies and slowed to a stop…just in time.

That behavior at an age when I should have known better is called foolish stubbornness. Fear didn't join in on the fun until I neared the bottom of what seemed to be a long hill. Our kids were skiing hard, trying to catch me, hoping to prevent disaster. We all gathered at the bottom, and they quickly asked, "Are you okay?" "Of course, I am just fine!" Aging tends to provide numerous examples where we are determined to prove that we can do whatever it is that we want to do…which is not always the case. Not every situation may be as dramatic or foolish as this example, but you know what I mean. I can do what I want to do!

I am growing older. My reflexes are no longer as quick. My arms can't lift as much, my legs can't run as fast, and I am better off sharing a hug with our grandson rather than arm wrestling. My pride jumps into action- Don't tell me I can't do that!

I should have known better than to go flying down a Blue Diamond slope. I should have made a wiser decision than needing to prove I still had a bit of Wonder Woman in me. I needed a reminder right then that my physical strength was not up to doing what it used to do. Time to be thinking wisely about my decisions.

ANOTHER OLD STORY

I have been sharing stories about a couple older gentlemen in the Old Testament. One doesn't read much about women involved in these very old stories, but I have always been impressed with two 'quiet' women who must have relied on their inner strength in order to move forward as they did.

Sarah, a beautiful young girl who was married to Abraham, brings one back to the immigrants I mentioned earlier. Sarah was young, and her husband told her that they were going to be moving to places unknown to them. God had a plan for Abraham, but there was nothing in the plan about Sarah other than she was going to be traveling with him.

I don't know how physical strength would have played out for women during this time. To do what they did, day after day, simply required outer strength. That must have been a given. But I think inner strength is different. Inner strength is what gets one through whatever the challenge might be, whatever the circumstances, and whatever the fear of the unknown might be…Sarah was able to manage her life journey.

Sarah was strong on the inside…Genesis doesn't record that she questioned Abraham about leaving her family. There are no words to tell about her response to Abraham using Sarah to protect his own well-being. I can appear strong on the outside, doing what must be done, but my inner strength is different. Inner strength holds my very being together during the most difficult of times. Inner strength keeps me focused on the path, focused on how to deal with the unknown.

Another woman by the name of Ruth made up her mind to do what seemed the best for her to do after the death of her husband. The women in Ruth's family seem to have had a close relationship, and they all understand the difficulties of being widows. During the time when Ruth lived, life was not easy for women after the death of a husband.

I don't know what Ruth thought about when her mother-in-law informed her two daughters in law that she would return to her own people in their land. She wished these women well as they moved on to whatever they chose to do. Ruth made her decision. "I am going with you." Ruth was beginning a new journey that she had never walked that she had not walked. Inner strength. She was moving to an area that had not been her home. She was leaving what she had known to start a life as a widow that would be difficult. She must have felt trust in following her mother-in-law even though this was most certainly a jog off her life path. I don't know what Ruth looked like, but just thinking about the choices she made, difficult choices for women during this time...I know for certain that she, as did Sarah, had a strong inner core that supported and encouraged the decisions she made.

Inner strength is more difficult to see as compared to our outer being. These women had additional choices to make as life continued, but at this point in their lives, I admire their inner strength. I wonder when I read about the age of people during this time period, but nevertheless, these women lived a long life. I was just as sure that the inner strength we read about regarding these experiences – that same inner strength continued to lead and guide them for the many years ahead.

Oh, I know our outer appearance seems important. I know my face looks different when I am over tired. I know extra weight isn't good for my heart. I know that the onset of some wrinkles gives others an idea of my age. But...readers, this isn't what growing older is about. My inner strength is what will support me when I hear the diagnosis of a serious illness. My inner strength is what will guide me when I mourn the loss of someone dear to me. My inner strength will keep me together when I realize that my age has changed my abilities, and I can no longer live alone. When these life events happen it doesn't matter if my wrinkles have been magically removed or my hair shows not one sign of being gray. My exterior is just along for the ride. My inner strength is the core that holds me up. Others might not actually see that part of me, but trust me, it is the part of me that will be that gold nugget for my aging journey. I can't purchase it in a fancy jar in the cosmetics aisle, nor can I exercise enough to keep me fit...inner strength is fed by something much deeper. Remember when I previously wrote that God promised to be with me always...well, that is inner strength.

Lord,

The older I become, the more challenging are those physical things I need to do. It seems I am asking for help more often. Can you reach this for me? Will you lift that for me? The yard work is just too much, even though I really do want the flowers by my house. I just get tired.

I watch others (a bit younger than I am) do so many things. I read about women who run marathons and climb mountains. Some days when I am cleaning my house, I end up feeling as though I have run and climbed all day.

Some days I don't want to admit to limitations. Somedays, I don't want to think about how I look. Somedays, I just get tired of thinking about what might be ahead on this aging thing.

Lord,

I know I am complaining. I will stop because I also know, for sure, that what is on the outside isn't what will get me through the days and years that are ahead. You have given me guidance over the years as to how to keep my inner strength strong as that of an Olympic athlete. You have provided a gold medal for a life of being strong within – a feat I could never have accomplished myself.

Lord,

I need to continue maintaining my inner strength so that we can, together, travel this journey. Help me to trust when I feel myself questioning; help me understand when life doesn't seem to make sense, and guide me in knowing how to have a peaceful heart as I take those steps over the tangled roots that just might appear on my path.

Lord,

I know I want to look good but remind me often that it's feeling good on the inside is what will get me home!

SOMETHING FOR YOU TO DO…

Thinking of ways we can become involved in this process is difficult because some of these experiences of aging are difficult. Inner strength is one of those topics, and I think the way to challenge yourself is to be still. Do you ever watch a squirrel run from here to there, jumping from tree to tree, demanding food at the bird feeder? Squirrels never seem to stop. And then I laugh because, after all their work collecting nuts and seeds, I wonder if squirrels even remember where they stored all that stuff.

I can relate to that squirrel. On the go all the time. Maybe that is why I am aware of the difference now … I am slowing down. My clean house and my busy calendar, and my always saying 'yes' when something was needed have changed. That is the part of me that others see on the outside. That is the part of me that just might cause others to wonder if I am feeling okay because I am not always doing something.

I am doing something. I am working on my inner strength. The strong outer woman is wearing down, but that doesn't mean that my heart and soul are not stronger than ever. Others might not see me when I say a prayer for my grandson. Others might not notice when I sit at my table and write cards to friends who are leading quiet lives as well. Friends, no marathons on my schedule, and just a touch of wrinkle-free cream on my face…but the inner part of me is alive and well.

SO, THINK ABOUT THIS…What is keeping you strong within? What is feeding the wisdom you need as you are growing older? Don't be embarrassed if you admit to a nap in the afternoon. Don't feel guilty if you say 'no' to a request. This is a time for you…a time for you to feed that inner part that provides the wisdom to do what we have to do as we grow older. I really don't know what all of that will be but it is my inner strength that will get me there.

Was it Wheaties that was called the Breakfast of Champions? Find that 'food' that will fill your soul so that on the journey, no matter how quickly or slowly you take those steps, on that journey you will be the champion with inner strength.

DO YOU KNOW THE WORDS…BE STILL AND KNOW THAT I AM GOD? IT'S A GOOD TIME TO BE STILL AND LISTEN TO THOSE WORDS. YOU WILL RECEIVE THE INNER STRENGTH YOU NEED.

AND WHILE YOU ARE BEING STILL…

Find a comfortable place to sit. Don't lie down, as you just might take a nap instead. Empty yourself of all the troublesome parts of this day. Don't focus on all that you did not get done. Don't add to your list all there is to do tomorrow. Right now, this moment just thinks of it as 'emptying the garbage.' It is just you, in a comfortable chair, in a quiet place…and we are ready.

A bit of background…there have been times when my head/my life has been too full to be healthy. If you knew me, you might be able to visibly identify those times. I might be too chatty, too obsessed with what I am doing, or maybe too quiet with all my concerns being chucked within. You know how you look or feel when there is just a bit too much going on in your life…even at our age!

This is a relaxation technique that has been popular for a long while. I even used this when I went to the dentist for one of those less-than-fun visits. No one will know what you are doing because it simply appears that you are closing your eyes and being quiet for a minute or two. But…that is not the case because you are traveling to your favorite place. The place that absolutely fills your heart and soul. The place that most certainly will even get you through that visit at the dentist!

Breathe. Breathe deeply. Begin to gather up what you need to travel to that perfect place. It might be your garden, just outside your front door. It might be in that fishing boat, out on the lake. Myy favorite place is a certain large rock, perfect for sitting, at our vacation spot in Maine. i can see it now! Leave all your responsibilities behind. Breathe. Breathe deeply. And imagine all that is around you. And then…think about your inner self. Think about what you need to fill your heart right now. Think about what is happening in that inner self. And then just be still and listen. Remember what I said, "Be still and remember just who it is that is God." You aren't alone. And when you are ready, come on back to where you really are. Remember to do this frequently!

THIS IS A SLOW ENDING TO THIS SECTION…

Here it is, another blank page. This is your inner strength page. When I am with friends someone frequently mentions the title of an especially good book. I usually forget the title by the time I get home. Or maybe I read about a movie that I just must see. Names are something I forget so easily. I might have heard a piece of music that was so relaxing. Ask Alexa what that title is.

This space is to dot down the most relaxing things that can fill your soul today. Don't belittle yourself for the things you can't do…slow down and remember the things that talk to your Inner Strength. Breathe.

ORDINARY…NOT ME or YOU

It was one of those nights when I was too restless to even fall asleep. After a couple hours of lying awake, I finally got up and puttered around a bit (someone asked me what 'puttering around' meant: It's what I do when I don't know what to do). My husband and the cat were sleeping soundly, so I quietly went downstairs, where my artwork space was located.

We chose our home because of its 'growing older' conveniences. We live in an area with hills and valleys and our flat driveway is a real bonus. The laundry and bedrooms are all on the main floor. There is just one step before one is outdoors. Blessings for growing older. The downstairs is another bonus that I quickly claimed as my own space. If they don't mind my numerous art projects here and there, I am quite happy to share this space with my husband and the cat!

It is the wee hours of the morning and sleep is not going to be my friend tonight so I might as well work on something. I completed a small weaving and worked on a drawing that will be a part of this book. The cat has wandered down to check on me but doesn't seem too concerned as he curls up on the sofa, eyes closing. I joined him, sitting close by, and a thought came to my mind.

I began looking around the room. It was like a life story of who we are…another memory lane experience. As I wrote previous pages for this manuscript, I frequently used the term 'ordinary.' Somehow, looking at all the things sitting around this room, my memories were most certainly not ordinary.

You and I…we are not ordinary. No one has walked in our shoes or dreamed our dreams. No one has awakened during the night to wander through a dark house, thinking my thoughts. We are each unique as we live our lives. I would guess there are other aging people who have been teachers and I know for certain that people in our neighborhood are our age. And friends with whom we share good times have celebrated as many birthdays as we have. BUT…not one of you, not you nor me, are ordinary. We are unique, one-of-a-kind gifts who live each day in the best way possible.

Okay, now I am really awake. My eyes move to a beautifully framed pen and ink drawing of Mont St. Michel. Years ago, I included art history in my art classes and one story I told my students was my dream to visit this particular place. One year I offered my high school students the opportunity to travel to France with an education program. What an experience with these young people. One of the sites on our tour was a visit to the Louvre. There we were in the midst of one masterpiece after another.

Somehow, someone in the group discovered that my husband and I were celebrating our wedding anniversary that very day. That evening a student came to our door and asked if we could come to their room. One of her room-mates was upset about something, and she needed our help. So we followed her to their room, and there, as we opened the door, was a gathering of smiling travelers holding a very large wrapped package. "Happy Anniversary!" and the "Open it!"

And we did. I don't know how they managed to carry this back to the hotel, but as the wrapping fell away, there was the incredible drawing of Mont St. Michel. We loved the gift, and for all the years since, it has hung on a special wall in our various homes. There is nothing ordinary about that very touching experience and the place of importance it still has in our home.

The travel around the room continued. Sitting along the wall where that drawing is hanging is an old ornate chest. There is one small handle missing, but that is just fine. The piece of furniture is beautiful. My mother-in-law so enjoyed antiques, and she had found this piece dirty and covered with chicken droppings. She must have seen possibilities under this mess as she took it home and preformed miracles. Both on the same wall - it and Mont St. Michel go together well.

I continue remembering. Hanging nearby is a calligraphy piece I created while in graduate school. Do you remember I shared that my grades in my first year of college left something to be desired? Eventually, I attended graduate school! You must be kidding!

There are several book shelves filled to overflowing with one book after another. Topics from Art to history, mysteries, and works by favorite authors. Some books I have even read twice. I remember buying the bookshelves at IKEA, thinking that we had a real connection with Scandinavia! In the spaces in front of the books, where space allows, are small treasures. A rock from the ocean shore. A tiny ceramic piece our daughter created in elementary school. An ornate little owl that a friend brought back from a visit to Russia. Treasures. And, of course, many spaces are filled with family photos from a variety of years and places.

As I sat there taking all this in, one memory after another, I could picture the story behind each experience or object. No, there is nothing ordinary about my life. Everyday experiences, one after another, make us who we are. Only when we miss the moment or ignore the event do we let an experience seem ordinary.

Maybe you have celebrated one of those special decade birthdays, as I call them. Maybe you have held a brand-new grandchild in your arms and experienced a love you can't begin to explain. Maybe you have taken that special vacation for which you saved and planned over a long period of time. And then there was that first day of not having to get up and go to work…retirement. No, there is nothing ordinary about how we have lived our lives.

You don't have to spend a sleepless night remembering and cherishing all those memories. Take a minute to just hold one of those special treasures as you dust your bookshelf. Share a piece of your story as someone tells you about their experience. Look at that photo taken years ago, but you knew it was special, and there it is, looking back at you, filled with memories.

Oh, it is so easy to feel ordinary. As I read about all the accomplished individuals in the world, I can't imagine what it would be that I have contributed to the life circle. They have invented, created and researched so many things that have made a difference in all of our lives. They are the biggest and the brightest. When I get in the mood to compare myself with others, I set the bar very high.

Come on! There is no such thing as an 'ordinary' person. For those of us on this aging journey, consider all that we have experienced. As a teenager, I never could have imagined the experiences that were ahead. Let me tell you, there has been nothing ordinary about the many decades I have lived. Sure, there are aches and pains. Concerns and fears. It's just natural. Changes we hadn't expected. Of course.

But…ordinary…not you and not me!

Ordinary seems to mean to me that anyone can do it. Not so…your smile was special when you met that stranger in the parking lot. They looked as though it was not a good day. Sending a thank-you note or a get-well wish was just what the receiver needed. A small surprise for that shut-in down the street. That all sounds so ordinary, but believe me…it is not; not for you nor for the person who is gifted by your thoughtfulness. It's all about remembering others and sharing just a small moment of yourself with them.

No, you are not ordinary. You are unique in being just who you are as a most special person. Don't argue with me. It's true! As you continue growing older, think about the ordinary. Think about what that means for you and the opportunities that are on your path. Think about what you are modeling for the younger generation. It is all anything but ordinary. If we aren't rich and famous by this point in our lives, I don't think it is going to happen. If we haven't accomplished amazing feats by now, I don't think it is going to happen. But do you know what…at this very moment, you are as special and unique as anyone on the planet. No one has walked in your shoes, nor are they going to. Be who you are and be the best at it as you can be.

Ordinary…not me! Not you!

There is a space here for you to describe one aspect of yourself that you often reflect on when you are feeling 'ordinary' and then consider how you can dump those thoughts and celebrate who you really are! So, first, think about what that one thing might be. Think about it for a bit. Write about it. And then turn that ordinary part of you into something you can celebrate. How can that work when it seems so very ordinary? Actually, I don't know what direction you will choose as you consider this part of who you are.

Maybe this will help. I remember my years as an art educator. There were other women who had jobs where they traveled to amazing places and some who made wonderful salaries or others who worked in fine high-rise office buildings where they went to work dressed in the finery of a real professional. What about those who chose various fields of medicine.

I was 'just a teacher.' (That's the first step.) Now you are going to explore equally unique aspects of being a teacher. Not 'just' a teacher. Think of the children with whom I interacted. Think of sharing the amazing journey of creativity with those kids! And the opportunities to explore my own creativity. Summer vacations when I could rest and work. There was nothing ordinary about my choice of vocations. Whatever it is that we chose to do, we were not ordinary in what we did or who we were.

WORDS FROM AN OLD BOOK

There had been many days of creating, and God was pleased with the results,

"And then God said, let us make mankind in our own image, in our likeness …"

And God saw that it was all very good.

Can it be any better than that? We are surely not ordinary!

God led the people to do many things on their various journeys. So many wonderful old stories where very common, ordinary people did extraordinary things. These were people who sometimes fell away from God's plan, who sometimes thought they knew best for themselves, and who somethings forgot what the plan was to be…in other words, these ordinary people went on to accomplish just what was needed. These ordinary people, who were often older when God needed them, stepped up to meet the challenge.

As I looked at all the treasures on my book shelves and the pictures on the wall, I stopped to also remember some of the 'ordinary' things I have done that, hopefully, that has made a difference. It's just fine to be ordinary! And in being the ordinary people we are…we can become the best that we can be!

Lord,

It's another day. Nothing special. Just an ordinary day. That's the way I feel sometimes.

Help me remember there is nothing ordinary about the sun coming up every day! There is nothing ordinary about all those things that grow, drop their seeds and once again come to life. There is nothing ordinary about all the years I have lived.

Lord,

I am one of the ordinary people in your extraordinary world. Sometimes, I wish that I could win that huge lottery prize or maybe even the *Publisher's Clearing House Award*. I sometimes wish that I was the best at something, anything. But here I am, just pretty ordinary.

Lord,

If you created centipedes and alligators, dragonflies and elephants, dandelions and oak trees…and thought they were all special, then I know you had something really good in mind when you created humankind.

Lord,

As I live my day, remind me you didn't mess around with anything ordinary. Everything you made was 'mind-blowing' amazing, and I am one of those extraordinary pieces in your plan. Thank you for making me 'out of the box' ordinary.

YESTERDAY, TODAY, AND TOMORROW

Do you remember the television quiz show where contestants were called to the stage to choose a numbered door, hoping there would be a prize behind that door? There was much thinking about the choice by both the contestant and the excited audience. Which door would be chosen!

These doors that I am describing are unique – different, much more carefully chosen. If you recall, the television program gave away wonderful prizes such as a cruise or maybe a new car. My game, where I am pretending to be on stage, is not about those kinds of prizes. My game (not really a 'game') also has three doors with signs above the door frames, each one containing a number and a word. I look out at the audience. There were three sections in the crowd…each one also had a word by the front seats linking that particular group to one of the three doors. Section One was generally quite young, and many of them I recognized as people I had known from my teaching jobs, from the neighborhoods where we had lived, family friends, and people close to our family. The sign over their area read *yesterday*.

The people in section Two were also familiar, maybe even more so. There were people seated here who we a part of my life right now. They were pretty much my age except for those friends who we are just beginning the aging journey. There was a lot of encouragement and clapping from this crowd. Their group displayed a sign with the word, *'Today.'*

And finally, Group Three. I didn't know anyone in this section. Some appeared to be dressed for work, and others were quite casual, as though they were maybe on vacation or puttering around their yard. None of them were doing too much hard labor. Some of them seemed quite elderly, and others appeared to be challenged with health concerns. No familiar faces. Their sign read *TOMORROW*. No one was clapping in this area, more just listening and watching. I don't think they knew me and didn't appear to know what was happening. I didn't understand their attitude.

The announcer began, hoping to get the audience involved in my considerations of which door to choose. "Think carefully. Which door are you going to choose? People in the audience began to cheer. The announcer asked, "Would you like Door One?" That section seemed very exciting.

127

"Choose our door!" Several people called out, "You remember me, don't you?" Some even knew my name!

"Next choice, my dear lady! Which one will it be?" The people in the Tomorrow section sat very quietly and sedately with questioning looks on their faces. The anticipation music began…you know, that kind of music that puts you on the edge of your chair! I had been told I could have as much time as I needed to choose.

I found it difficult to let go of Yesterday. I have so many good memories. I kept looking back at that door. There were vacations, family events, and experiences that brought new beginnings. *Door One* – it was tempting.

I moved on to consider *Door Two*. This is all about what is happening in my life right now. No surprises. Not really memories, as it is all continuing to be a part of who I am. Everyone in this group is pretty much focused on what is on their plate right at this moment. It's like listening to the voice on my GPS and knowing just where to go. Clean, clear, and comfortable! Familiar!

My husband corresponds with a fellow student from my college days. Daryl was an exceptional student…one of those great test-takers and note-writers. Daryl took education seriously. He has been involved with a lot of different life journeys. He has been busy with anything that would keep him busy. Daryl is a thinker. We received a letter from him recently, and he shared a bundle of thoughts about memories and those things from yesterday. He was remembering family, his wife, and when his children were young. There had been ups and downs, but there was also unconditional love for his wife and children. The years had been a learning time about growing into adulthood. Their working years passed, and so did any thought about who they had been or were becoming. He had ideas about easing off this workload and making changes as he was rather casually experiencing growing older. Daryl had been a part of our experiences yesterday, and it was difficult to ignore this group as they were beginning to cheer me toward choosing *door two*.

Sometimes we feel as though we are the kind of people who need to hang tight to yesterday. I have even kept some of our daughter's cute baby clothes. No one is ever going to wear them again. Memories have the potential to be quite comforting as time moves on. It's kind of the feeling of security that one doesn't want to let go. I guess I could call it 'familiar security.'

But there is still one more door. Remember the one door left where the audience has me wondering if I even want to consider what might be behind their door? I have listened to the announcer and heard the cheers of the audience, and I kind of feel that the choice is not really up to me. This group is totally unfamiliar and is so quiet, almost disinterested. There is something so unknown about this final door. It's as though I have no map to show me the way, no advice from someone who has walked through this door.

Okay, I am going to choose *Door One*. Familiar. Lots of smiles from people I remember. After all, we need memories. I am thinking back to my description of the rain tub with the overflow of memories. Who is going to join me as I continue the journey through the winter of my years? If I choose *yesterday*, I don't know that I am really going to have a sense of completing my journey. I reflect on those memories…and slowly move on to Door Two.

A few tears later and I am at the next door. This is a tough decision. The audience is impatient. TODAY…it has turned out to be good times. I'm healthy and have the energy to do what I need to do. I enjoy time with friends and love being involved with all the goings on with family. TODAY is good, but it sometimes tricks me. I have alluded to, in other parts of my book, things that I can no longer do comfortably or safely. It is those fitted sheets that are so hard to tuck under the mattress. And driving at night. Really, I am healthy, but it is those things that are beginning to challenge me. I have had hip and knee replacements and they were wonderfully successful, but I am still not signing up for down-hill ski lessons. Okay, walk by that door.

But I need to continue. If my journey is to continue, I need to at least consider DOOR THREE. Spring and summer have been good experiences, and autumn was relaxing and quite pleasant. I don't know anything about winter. I don't know if I can manage the strong winds blowing in my direction. What if I can't deal with the cold temperature? After all, it's winter.

Again, the announcer said that it was time to choose. "Which door will it be?" I hold my breath. Can I let go of *yesterday*? Am I able to move on from what today has to offer? i don't know anything about tomorrow. But the game is waiting…my choice is needed. I surprise the audience by choosing D*oor Three*! i can tell they are surprised. That's okay. We are each on our own journey. Some of us aren't ready to leave yesterday behind. That's okay. Move at your own pace. Others are still so busy being involved in today. It's not easy to set aside those things that are currently what keep us busy.

But *Door Three*…I had to think carefully. This prize was not about a cruise or a new car. This was about what I need to learn on my journey as I am growing older. I can't just stay in the past and wish all that was back in my life. When I consider what today has to offer, it seems that things are rushing past me. I can't keep up.

It takes courage to consider the unknown. To make a choice to step over the threshold of *Door Three*. Seems reasonable – many of us don't look forward to winter. But whether I am eager for winter or not, it is going to come. I am going to step out into the colder temperatures, and I will feel the bite of the wind. I am already experiencing winter. I can do this. I make my choice. I want to be able to move forward in a way that I am not fearful of what is ahead. I want to be able to be strong enough to explore what it is that I do not know. I want to be able to be wise enough to understand change and move on. I want to have fun with remembering and keeping some memories. I want to be able to have the courage to step over the threshold of *Door Three,* and greet winter with gusto. "Winter, I am ready. Here I am. How about if I take you on with a good snowman-building contest."

I can do this. So can you.

Door Three is a good choice. Winter, here I come! But remember, the journey of getting there is not a journey you will travel alone.

Lord,

I have lived such a long life. There was the satisfying spring and summer of my journey. Growing up and decision making. Some of that was a challenge. I learned a lot along the way.

Lord,

All that learning and growing. I suppose everyone goes through what seems like a lot of years managing all that we have to do to maintain the life we are living. I hope I have made a difference as I traveled my journey through yesterday and today. Help me be ready for tomorrow.

Lord,

Gray hair, a body that is slowing down, and a few snow flurries in the air. The seasons have been a pleasure. It wasn't always easy, but I am thankful that you remained close to my heart.

Lord,

I have lived a long life. You have provided so many blessings along the way. Now I am catching the snowflakes that are beginning to fall. Some melt in my hand, and others begin to gather in bunches on the ground. Winter is going to stick around. Give me courage and inner strength, insight, and wisdom as I move forward. I know that I will always walk being protected through whatever might seem to be a storm. Keep me warm!

MORE OLD STORIES...

Have you ever considered how much was accomplished throughout the many pages of Scripture and all that was done without the technology we have available today?

God didn't provide a map quest for Abraham and Moses. So many years of traveling. What courage and fortitude they must have had. Abraham was challenged by leaders along the way, not knowing for sure what was going to be happening to he and Sarah. Nevertheless, they plodded along, following the plan God shared with them. Abraham sometimes took things into his own hands, and I don't know if those decisions were the best for them. But the two of them hung in there.

And then there was Moses. You remember from another section how Moses worked with the Israelites. There was traveling. Always the journey in front of them. Maybe that is a good reminder for us. The journey is going to be there. How we prepare is the question. They were not just taking a vacation trip to the ocean or the mountains. It was forty years of walking and walking and walking. There was complaining. But they continued...

Abraham and Moses spent longer than a lifetime searching and wandering. They experienced fear and frustration, anger and trials. They knew love for the people they were guiding, and both men understood the importance of the love God had for them.

I complain about my aches and pains. I don't think there is a birthday cake large enough for all the candles Abraham and Moses would have needed, but then, I am right behind them. God needed both of these people, and God needs you and me. We are part of the plan even if we are entering the months of winter. What memories they must have had as they sat down at the dinner table with their friends and shared stories.

And then winter came for both of these men, and they were blessed.

JESUS SAID, "KNOCK, AND THE DOOR WILL BE OPENED. Lord, guide us to be wise as we choose our way on this journey. Give us the courage to choose the right door and then the boldness to step over the threshold with courage.

SOMETHING FOR YOU TO DO...

So, what more can I say about choice and change, about remembering and forgetting? I have shared stories of experiences that have been a part of who I am. Others have shared pieces of their stories. I like the idea of the reader being involved in what they are reading, so here is another thing to try.

Using a piece of copy paper, fold it tri-fold...however, you can make that work for you. The idea is that you are dividing your paper into three sections. And, as you might have guessed, somewhere, write the words, one word in each third of the paper – *YESTERDAY, TODAY, AND TOMORROW*.

Each of us has thoughts related to those words. Maybe you could relate to some of my ideas. But we have traveled on different journeys and carried different baggage. Some of us have made wrong turns, while others have discovered interesting adventures. You might have even experienced both! For some, it is just too hard to leave yesterday. There are so many memories that seem to hold one back. Even stepping from yesterday into today can be challenging. It is simply a part of the struggles we experience as we move forward with our lives.

You might have moved through those days comfortably, step after step, and then bumped into a brick wall when you realize tomorrow is just around the corner. Maybe using that description makes the time pass too quickly, but tomorrow is definitely on our path.

We all experience times when life seems confusing and a bit unmanageable. There are times when we keep those rose-colored glasses on more than necessary, and we miss reality. It's kind of like the weather...one day sunny and the next two, cloudy and gray. The weather might even bring a storm or two as well as picture-perfect days. This is how life goes on.

What we need to be able to do and to understand is that, even with those ups and downs, what is important is that we pause, ponder, and proceed with wisdom and guidance, knowing we are not entering the new day alone.

It is a challenge. When someone has a birthday at my age, there is a joke shared frequently, "Oh, you are thirty-nine again!" No, that isn't going to happen, but instead of the black balloons and party decorations, gently celebrate the journey you have made so far. Recognize the challenges. Cheer on all the fun stuff. Just remember to be real in the process. Aging is inevitable. You won't have fewer candles on your cake next year. Don't focus on '39 again' but try to think more along the lines of live, laugh and love…to the best of your ability.

Consider those three sections.

Yesterday – have you had a letter from an old friend, or maybe a phone call? Pets become a part of the family, and loss of a special pet can be devastating. Did a dear friend move to be closer to adult children? Or it might be that you attended a class reunion and what a great time…trying to remember the names of those kids who were your best buddies.

Today - Right now, we are all living in today. There are still responsibilities and appointments. Lunch with friends and maybe a card game on the weekends. It is also about remembering to take our medicine and check your blood pressure. Today is all about living in the moment. Living in the moment can mean so many different things. If you have lost a loved one, today can be lonely. If you are experiencing health concerns, today can be frightening. If you are planning that cruise I mentioned, you are probably busy packing just the right clothes. Whatever is happening today is being in the moment. We are all unique, and that moment is going to be different for each of us. Another piece of being in that moment might include a bit of envy. Your friend is up and about, doing everything someone ten years younger would be doing. Doesn't seem fair! No, it probably doesn't. Have you thought about how you will deal with this bit of envy? Talk it over with someone. You will feel much better, and your friendship won't suffer.

Tomorrow - Here is that door of the unknown. Do you have any plans? Are you thinking about what you can do to make the days one of sunshine rather than stormy? Are you going to need assistance on the rest of this journey? Can you make plans on your own would it be good to reach out to someone? Don't put off those plans for tomorrow because tomorrow will come. Don't ignore today what you can do to help tomorrow by the best kind of day.

I'm not trying to treat any one of those days lightly. There will be both ups and downs every day. Take some time and fold up that paper and think about what life has shared with you on each of those days…not literally but during the different times in your life. What has passed, what is happening now, and how the future might look. Whatever the day you are considering, don't miss the gifts that were put into your life, and don't be fearful of dealing with the challenges that might have changed your life.

Now…go find that sheet of paper and get to work!

I WAS JUST THINKING:

After talking about yesterday, today, and tomorrow…I got thinking about calendars. I like the time of the year when school supplies are on the shelves. Just the smell of new crayons and all the colors of notebooks and fun backpacks cause me to be on overload. I always recognize parents of beginning school children walking with their school needs lists, checking everything off. That is authentic excitement. I watch and am excited with them!

School sales generally include calendars. I just have to buy a new calendar! I usually choose one that has a space for every moment of my life and stickers as a bonus. It's got to be big! And I work to find a big calendar, but then what happens is that it is so big it becomes cumbersome, and I don't even use it. I just don't have that much happening in my life. I forget to use the stickers, or else, lose them.

But think about this. Search for a calendar that has your name on it. Not literally, but you know what I mean. One that really speaks to you, and then use it. Keep it someplace where you remember where you put it. Hey, maybe you should keep your keys with your calendar! Deciding where to keep a calendar might also encourage me to organize my desk, which tends to be somewhat of a disaster. Remember that rain tub…well it flows over onto my desk as well.

Actually, with the possibilities available on your computer, you could create your own personal calendar. So what is a calendar for, you ask? A calendar is not just a week. A calendar is meant to help you remember what happens in your life on that particular day of the week. A calendar is meant to help you remember the dates of your friends' birthdays. A calendar is not like a scrapbook with a billion pages, including stickers. A calendar is a calendar – a tool to make life less complicated on a day-to-day basis. So, basically, what I need is a simple calendar.

Here we go again…with the pieces of aging coming together. Organizing, remembering, forgetting…all those things we do as we grow older. You have no doubt heard the saying, "You can't teach an old dog new tricks." I would disagree. Dogs are smart and ready to learn something new at any point in their life. I might have been disorganized in the yesterday and today or my life, but guess what – I can learn to manage these days in a more organized manner. Did it really take gray hair on my head to realize that even I can become organized!

When you can't remember from yesterday to today and don't want to think about tomorrow…breathe. Think. Be sensible. Do little things that will help on this aging journey. I wondered if I should buy that new drug, Prevnogen but then decided it would be wiser and more practical to clean off the top of my desk and keep track of that new calendar.

SAYING GOOD-BYE

I made reference previously to how interesting it is that just when you become involved in something in particular, other related things begin popping up with a similar topic. A new magazine arrived in our mailbox, a free magazine as a trial, and the focus on the whole issue was 'aging.' I was reviewing sections of what I had written for this book, and in the background, Kenny Rogers was singing "It's Hard to Say Goodbye." (Remember Kenny Rogers?)He might have been singing about a broken relationship with a girl, but nevertheless, his words hit me right on! Saying good-bye. I am often reminded how difficult it is to say goodbye.

Years ago, my husband, daughter, and I would drive from Ohio to Minnesota during our vacation break to visit our families. We were young and involved in our work and responsibilities, so this was a once-a-year visit. The two weeks always passed quickly. On the morning of our departure from the homes of our parents, who were most certainly growing older, I knew both my husband and I were thinking, "Would we do this trip again, and would everything be the same?"

Our parents would begin their goodbyes. As we were leaving, usually my mother would be the one who would go through all the things we had not had time to do on this visit. There had been someone else to visit, and she hadn't had time to make the meal that she had planned. It was just easier to remember the undone things than to actually say goodbye…as though that could keep us a bit longer.

Isn't that life? We live a full life, and still life begins to change as we are reminded that there is still go much that 'needs' to be done. I don't know that it matters what evening we end our day; in our mind, there is something that we think, "Oh, I should have finished…" whatever that might be. Maybe it has something to do with the idea of a task being completed, finished, done…and after that, we say goodbye and move on. Sharing time with friends, doing something especially enjoyable, spending time on an interesting project…all the same concept. We don't want it to end. Moving on pulls a bit at our heartstrings.

As it was with our parents…our aging parents. What would next year bring in regard to our traditional visit home? Would we still vacation at the lake with my husband's family? Would my mother still be busy in her kitchen? Would my dad be mowing the lawn that seemed to get larger each summer? As those visits came to an end each summer, there were unspoken thoughts, never discussed aloud but in the minds of all of us. Instead of actually sharing our concerns, we shared hugs and some tears.

The times were a bit different in the mid-sixties. Our Scandinavian parents were more likely to keep such serious talk to themselves. We all were living in the moment. What my husband and I would wonder…when is that going to change. Even after a generation of families living in America and establishing American ways, there were things one just doesn't do. Talking about age and death with your children we off limits. Never do I recall any personal conversation as to what was on their mind about end-of-life choices.

Well, the inevitable did happen. One year, in the midst of a cold winter, we received a phone call. It was a heart attack. Yes, of course, we would make plans immediately. In a day, we were back in Minnesota participating in funeral plans. How quickly we realized as we made preparations that, no, we had not been there to say goodbye.

Travel to destinations all over the world has become so accessible. Employment has sent people to one corner of the world or another. New friends could have a conversation about growing up, and several different places could be described. We might chat about similar experiences on our individual journeys. Sometimes just describing my past to a new friend causes me to quickly realize the changes that have filled my growing older years.

Moves meant the younger generation was hither and yon while mom and dad remained 'at home'. Those who remained behind probably waited for those connections. However, they arrived…letters, phone calls, zoom meetings, texts – all were a means of staying in touch. The conversation might be about the goings on of the day of the week, and then eventually, one of them would say, "Well, I've got to go. I need to get back to work or the kids or make dinner. Love you. Bye!" At that moment, the connection ends.

For those of us who are growing older, saying good-by tugs at the heart strings even if it is just at the end of a phone call. I smiled, looking at old photos to see how many were taken standing by the car, saying goodbye. That time between visits can feel like a lifetime.

I mentioned that our grandparents left various parts of Scandinavia for America many, many years ago. They boarded a ship, and everyone knew that there were no plans to return to celebrate family birthdays. Saying goodbye at the pier and sharing a hug, was a sharing of love that would need to last forever. Kenny Rogers was still singing in the background as I thought about this departure. Parents were sending their children off to new lands across the ocean. Maybe a young son or husband was leaving to serve in the military, frightened as he left his family. Goodbyes had been said and the love in that hug was going to have to last a very long time.

Leaving what is familiar might be an exciting experience…or maybe not. Years of being employed usually led to retirement. That worker who is leaving has been doing their job by the side of a friend for so many years. Now that older worker is retiring and moving out of the area. A retirement part? A gold watch? A cake and lots of storytelling. And then it's time to move on. More hugs and handshakes. Picture taking. Come back to see us!" Then it is goodbye. Not easy.

The world has become smaller than when I was a kid. Experiences have grown into amazing adventures. Travel opportunities will allow me to go almost anywhere in the world. We have become a mobile generation. If this is going to be the case during my growing older years, as friends move for various reasons, I need to discover ways in which I can make my goodbye experiences more heart-filling and creative. The space between us widens…that might just be the way it is. That does not mean the friendship must end. That doesn't mean I forget loved ones. If I am thoughtful with my goodbyes, it will help ease the woes in my heart. I need to remember to fill my goodbye with a love that will help me to manage the loss I experience.

An interesting example happened to me recently. Over the period of months, we recognized that a dear family member was living her last days on this earth. In addition to being a family member, she and I were simply just good friends and had been for so many years. She would send long emails with all the pieces of their days and what was going on in their lives. Sometimes there were packages…often chocolates! Our families had vacationed together. Now we were sharing memories and stories with her husband. I was going to miss her.

Then a surprising thing happened. Her best friend, who lived near their home, reached out to me. She, too, was experiencing a great loss. They had done so much together. We introduced ourselves to each other and exchanged stories. Then she suggested that we carry on the friendship that had been shared between us as friends and relatives. Guess what! She sent a special box of chocolates at Christmas! Her letters and email are fun and chatty. We remember and tell stories. We both continue to recognize the empty space, but we share the memories and carry on traditions. An empty space can begin to be filled a little bit at a time.

Could we be more mindful of even the everyday goodbyes that touch us during ordinary experiences every day? An 'old' friend might be in a care center…I have time to share a phone call or send a card even though the miles between don't allow visits. Sharing a conversation about what's happening, talking about the nasty weather neither of us likes, checking on mutual friends…this makes the goodbye less difficult. A friend has just stepped into the role of a new widow. This is a time of feeling so empty and lost. She said, "Just call me so that I don't feel so alone." And what is more fun for a grandparent who lives miles and miles from a grandchild but they are able to visit face to face on their computers or telephones. Oh, the wonders of technology.

Saying goodbye is hard. I don't like that goodbyes have become more frequent as we grow older. It's become a reality for many of us ordinary folks. I tend not to hop on an airplane for an afternoon chat over a cup of coffee. I probably don't plan a cruise so that we can vacation together. It's more than I can manage with my age and finances. As many things might stand in the way of making the distance between us less, there are just as many that can encourage us to be creative as we keep the friendship alive.

I have shared serious aspects of saying goodbye, but in my memories, saying goodbye also leads to adventures. As I look back on adventures we experienced at a younger age, we were not only adventurous, but we also relied on a bit of courage. Two small-town kids moving out into new and unknown parts of the country. We were young…then. But here we are at an older age, experiencing some of the same unknowns, still requiring courage to move forward just a step at a time. New friends are made…and left. New jobs are started…and left.

As all these changes were happening, we began to realize that we were experiencing loss each time we made a change. We were no longer sitting around the table, chatting with friends, but we remembered! We remembered the memories. I'm not making light of these goodbyes, as every change leaves its mark. Each goodbye is different. Even so, it is important to process…and to be aware of the process…whether we are young and setting out on a new adventure or we are aging and realizing that we can no longer live alone.

As I thought about this aspect of aging, the various experiences of the aging process seemed to come together. Aging isn't just one kind of experience. We don't just all of a sudden become 'old'! We are like those huge oak trees in our yard or the flowers that brighten up the front of our house. We grow through stages. It doesn't happen all at once. We are a process. There is a goodbye that means there has been a loss, and that means there are memories. Life is a golden circle when we allow ourselves the thought that these are memories in the making.

We don't just become old. Aging isn't just a one-of-a-kind experience. We are like those huge oak trees in our yard. We all grow through a variety of stages. We are a process happening. There is a goodbye which means that there has been a loss, and that means there are memories. And on and on the life cycle goes. Life is a golden circle when we allow ourselves to be a part of that whole process. Ignoring the fact that we are growing older just won't work. I'm not saying that this whole process comes without challenges and some fears, but ignoring what is happening will simply add to the confusion and frustration of all the changes.

Maybe the place in which we are at this moment is meant to lead us into the open arms of yet another step in the process. If I open myself to feeling the grief of a loss, I can begin to explore the memories. We slowly accept the change that comes with saying goodbye. The key to the process is 'slowly' accepting what is happening in our life. We change – life changes – but the circle never changes. Piece by piece, it will all come together.

ANOTHER OLD STORY

God had an eye on a man in a distant land. (You have read about these folks in a previous section) As usual, God had a plan in mind. This man was quite ordinary, as I understand from what I have read, but he was about to become a very unique piece of God's Big Picture Plan.

Abram was his name, and Sarai was his wife. Eventually, both of their names would change, so you might be more familiar with Abraham and Sarah. These folks, along with a couple other family members, were invited by God to do some traveling. They were to leave the home that was familiar to them and move on to a place that they knew nothing about. Again, as with other travelers about whom we have read, they would not be returning for family reunions.

God said, "Abram, I have an extensive plan in mind, and I really need your assistance. This is going to be a long-term adventure, so you will need to say goodbye to your families. I don't know when you might be together again. Such an ordinary couple these two were, but this was about to be the beginning of quite an experience.

Everything was packed. Not the difficult part of the preparations, as now it was time for Abram and Sarai to say goodbye to all that was familiar. Abram might have been assured that God was not going to leave them alone, but that didn't make the goodbyes any easier. Leaving what we know or losing someone we love is difficult at best.

When I become involved in those goodbyes that are especially difficult, I need to learn and understand that this is a part of the process. Good-bye is not just the words exchanged at the time of the change or the loss. It carries with it feelings for the long term. As trying as the next step might be…this is where I open myself to what is ahead. Closing down often leaves the circle broken. Reaching out to hold the hand of the person on each side of you will give you the strength and courage for whatever the process presents. Abram had no idea that he would meet kings and become exceeding wealthy. He couldn't have imagined the events in which he would participate. Abram probably had not heard about the concept of 'one step at a time,' but that was about what happened to he and Sarah on their journey. When Sarai said to Abram, "Why did we ever leave our home and family?" he probably reached out to her and said, "I know what you mean, but God made a promise, and I am going to go with the promise." There might be struggles for us, but God is not going to step out of the Circle of Life.

Lord,

Life seems to always be changing faster than I can manage to keep up. We seem to be saying goodbye to someone too often. And if it isn't a person, it is something to which I have become accustomed.

Lord,

Here I go again. I don't like to say goodbye. You sent your children to places far and wide throughout many generations. Each time you promised that you would not be the one saying goodbye to your people. You traveled right along with them, just as you promised.

Lord,

Goodbyes kind of start me thinking about the future as I grow older, and I don't know for sure what that future holds for me. I get a bit nervous sometimes. You know what is ahead, and you know when I feel anxious. I do know you made a promise, but I still don't like goodbyes.

Lord,

I am one of those people who need assurance that I am going to be able to do this aging thing. Help me remember that goodbyes are not forever when you are in my life. Wipe away the tears and calm the fears and remind me that you are 'forever.'

Lord,

For now, I am just going to wave and say 'thanks' for the care you shared with me all along this journey.

SOMETHING FOR YOU TO DO…

How can you begin to explore the process of growing older in your particular life? I don't like needing to consider that step any more than you do. I like pretending that I know how to play all those fast video games. I imagine that I can take a long hike without becoming winded. It might be easier to pretend to imagine that we are able to do something we really do know we can't do.

There are so many ways in which we can keep that circle of life important as we grow older. We need each one of us to be there for support as we begin to wander through this path of aging. When it is time so say good-bye for one reason of another we need to remember that there is an empty space in the circle that we simply can't ignore.

Years ago while I was a student, I learned a process called webbing. I have found it helpful as I try to figure out things that challenge my thinking. The idea is to draw a shape in the center of a sheet of paper. Within that shape I will write the main focus of what is on my mind. If I did that right now that word would be Aging.

Okay, now draw a straight line from that circle and then draw a smaller circle at the outside end of that straight line. In this smaller circle I am going to write the words for one aspect of growing older that is on my mind. One idea might be MY PHYSICAL HEALTH. Draw another line off in another direction and make another circle at the end of that line. Inside this circle write a different thought about aging…maybe DOWNSIZING. The words within the smaller circles will be different for each one of you…must make it personal to you! If you wish, and have a large enough paper, you can even make another line branching out from that smaller circle and continue your thought process even more specifically. Actually, that would be an excellent idea. Now go find some big sheets of paper.

Once that process has been completed to your satisfaction, sit back and look at what has developed. Sit back and think. What has been on your mind? What kinds of things are you ready to take on as you are growing older? Keep the paper on which you have been working. Add more webbing. Do more thinking. It's just a tool to help you consider what is important to you on that path ahead.

This isn't an assignment or a contract. It is a step in opening my mind as I deal with the ton of stuff that is rattling around. Who knows, the next time you look over your thoughts the circle might change. And what if you shared this process with a friend? So many possibilities when we open our minds to something new.

As you are managing this webbing process, think about some ideas that you try to ease your mind though the good-byes you have experienced.

•	Check out Google for a site where you could make a photo book. All those memories that are filling your heart maybe need a place to be where you can hold them and look at them. Creating a book is not difficult and the very process might be a healing experience.

•	You have said too many good-byes. It's time for you to do something that fills your heart rather than empty it. It's difficult to experience loss in any shape or form. Check out your treasures. Maybe you have a special book or a china dish…maybe it is a piece of jewelry you cherish. A good tool that has been special for many tasks. Whatever that item might be, let it go. Give it to someone who will understand the value of that treasure. I could share a beautiful feather with someone. It is when you see the expression on their face or hear their 'thank you' that you will be filled with the experience of giving something away rather just saying a good-bye.

SOME FINAL PIECES TO THE STORY...

"Happy Birthday to you...

Happy Birthday to you..."

And then the final line would be in harmony with the words *"And many more."*

Do you ever pause when you are involved with something special and think, "How many more times...?" I don't mean that in a negative way but rather just realistically thinking about the days ahead. Sometimes I don't really know how I should think about aging. Should I be focusing on all those boxes in the basement that need sorting? Should I be going through files and papers to be sure that all is in order? Or maybe I should be exercising and eating properly so that I stay healthy. I really don't know.

Life is so amazing. I look at tiny new babies, and it is a mystery how those little bodies grow and grow with every part knowing just what to do, and then one day, that tiny body is an adult. And what do we say, "I can't believe how you have grown!"

But the growth doesn't stop. Years may go by, and our physical selves might look pretty much the same. Height might vary. Facial features might change a bit. Hairstyles. Weight. During the younger adult years, friends could meet and probably recognize each other. There might be features that are even similar to those early features that you see in baby pictures.

Growing isn't just about our outward appearance. That outward appearance is who your parents watched grow into an adult. That outward appearance is who your friends see when you meet for lunch. That outward appearance is who, eventually, your own children recognize as mom and dad. That outward appearance is how we are known to others. We all have that outward physical appearance.

If you haven't already experienced the change, one day, you will look into the mirror and say to yourself, "That person looking back at me has lived a good long life. That person looking back at me has experienced one adventure after another. That person looking back at me has celebrated a lot of birthdays." Yes, indeed, that person has been on a life journey.

Life begins with that first breath the newborn takes. Life fills his/her lungs, and a cry calls out, "Here I am World!" The journey begins. That voice cries out numerous times over the years ahead. "Look at me. I can ride my bike without training wheels!" Look at me. I have my first job!" Look at me. I am celebrating my retirement." Until one day, we slow down and think, "My, where did all those years go?" And this is where I would like to walk with you as we near the end of our journey. It has seemed to pass quickly.

I think this is where that inner strength kicks in for real! More than one person has made a statement like, "Growing older is not for sissies!" "Growing older is not an easy job!" Right! Back to our inner strength. I look back on those brand-new babies and how much attention they required. Feeding, nurturing, leading, loving, and on and on. I remember the thrill of watching those first steps, hearing the excitement of a little voice as first grade began, fretting about wondering if we were doing the right things as parents, managing an empty nest, and then, the excitement of seeing our daughter begin the adventure of her own life.

The circle of life continues. I can look back on where the circles had beginnings generations and generations ago. I can remember growing up years on a farm in Minnesota, and then…my own personal adventure took flight. I didn't know that plan, nor did I check out on a map just where my destination would be. I don't know that any one of us can actually do that. I can make a plan and then work my way through the challenges and changes. I can focus on what seems to be the right path for me and then be willing to meet the challenges and changes. Challenges and changes. Hopes and dreams. Think back to the idea of a puzzle. So many pieces. Open the box. Tear open the bag with all the pieces, and as they are dumped out on the table, the puzzle looks impossible. I look at the box to check on the image one more time. I begin with one piece at a time.

First, I organized the pieces with like colors. Oh, and I need to find the pieces that will make the edges. Patience. Asking for some help. Taking a break and coming back with my eyes rested. Little by little, the pieces fall into place. Once in a while, I have to make some adjustments because the piece I chose was just not quite the right piece. What a difference it made to get that piece out of there.

Could it be that life is kind of like a puzzle? There are puzzles of all levels of difficulty and a variety of sizes. Some of us live lives that are organized and simple. Large pieces and a clear image to build on. If we are really feeling like stepping out, the number of pieces increases, as does the level of difficulty.

I arrived in this world much like that puzzle. At the onset, the level of difficulty in putting that life together is basically sorting out the pieces and finding those that are going to make the edges. Gradually a frame develops, and similar pieces begin to come together. The process varies for the person putting the puzzle together. Some seem to smoothly find one piece after another, while some struggle to the point of thinking that those pieces need to be put back into the box. Some of us reach out for some assistance, knowing this is more than we can handle on our own.

Life takes time, just as puzzles take time. Sometimes a piece gets lost or misplaced, and there is a bit of drama at to 'now what'!

And where am I going with this story?

Back to the concept of inner strength. Moving through life is kind of like that puzzle. We can't see the final product in the beginning. We might be a bit overwhelmed at times, thinking I just can't get all of this together. And then several pieces come together at once, and you call out those familiar words, "Look what I did!"

The life circle will provide a bushel basket of emotions and experiences. There will be exciting times that simply must be shared with others. There will be times when you want to just close your eyes and wonder how you could have made such a mistake. There will be rewards for moving forward as well as quiet times of disappointment. Some experiences will fill you to bursting with energy that doesn't stop, and other times, you will feel as though the bottom has dropped out. Some people will seem to live on easy streets, and others feel as though nothing has gone their way. Good health will be a wonderful bonus for some, and for others, the illness will zap the energy they had counted on.

Back to that inner strength.

It's what we have to go on. It is what will help us share the magic moments as well as provide what is needed when the disappointments are heavy on our shoulders. When illness presents us with problems we never expected, our inner strength helps us continue the journey, but it also opens us to the acceptance that we are not going to get through this on our own. Inner strength will give us guidance when we find ourselves traveling solo, losing a lifetime companion. Inner strength will provide us with courage when there seems to be no light at the end of the tunnel.

We had lunch with a group of friends. Conversation flowed with ordinary topics being shared. Then one individual mentioned something related to health concerns. Oh my, how quickly we all could relate. It seemed necessary to tell others about the incident that changed our own life. It's all-natural. Aging experiences seem to surround me at the moment. A friend is having surgery. Another friend has just learned that cancer will be her companion for the ongoing future. Others have a heavy heart as family concerns arise. If you think back to an earlier section of my book, you might remember that as I started writing, it seemed that topics related to aging were everywhere. Of course, it might have something to do with the fact that our friends are basically our age. We joke about those who are just 'spring chickens' in our group of friends. Of course, they can still climb the mountains and run the marathon. Not to worry…their day is coming! And on and on, we go chuckling as we give these 'kids' a hard time.

Aging. We just can't get around it. But…what we can do is live our life the best way we know how the best we are able. If my heart and soul are full, it doesn't matter whether I am on the golf course at sun up or sitting on the front porch with a blanket around my shoulder as I manage an illness. If my heart and soul are satisfied and nourished, it doesn't matter if I am on a cruise through the islands or am saving money for a trip to visit the grandkids. If my heart and soul are complete, so shall I be complete.

Is that easy? No, I don't think it is easy, but it certainly is possible. Are paths with more than my share of speed bumps the way I want to travel? I don't think so. If I know that the speed bumps are there, I will be ready. If I know that others share the same frustrations and cares, I will seek out their support as well as support them. We probably could travel alone, but that would be a long, quiet journey.

I shared a short verse about Hands in the beginning. Open yourselves. Those are helping hands. Reach out, and don't wait until the last minute. Be willing to give a hand as well as receive help from the hands of others.

How many times during these pages have I written, "Do you remember?" Here is one more. Do you remember the old song about the old lady who was fetching water, except there was a problem? The song goes like this,

"Oh, Liza,

Oh, Liza …there's a hole in your bucket, a hole in your bucket,

Yes, a hole in your bucket."

And poor Liza is not going to get home with any water if she has a hole in her bucket. I don't want us to continue on our journey with a hole in our hearts and soul. A hole where all the energy and desire and hope and joy are going to dribble out before we arrive home. Years ago, we had a car that developed a hole in the gas tank, which was not good. I was away from home when the patch fell off, so I patched it with a piece of chewed bubble gum. Not really a suitable patch, but I couldn't get home with a hole in such a critical place. We can't patch the significant holes in our hearts with something that will just not stick.

And my friends, if we are on this journey of aging, we can't travel safely with a hole in our hearts.

Oh, Liza, Oh Liza

There is a hole in your heart, a hole in your heart. Yes, a hole in your heart.

And Liza responds:

"A hole in my heart? How did that happen? What am I going to do?"

That is sort of what Liza said, but she realized that the hole was serious. The hole needed mending.

The journey on which we are embarking, this time of growing older, can be filled in so many different ways, but if there is a hole in our hearts, we aren't going to be able to keep much in our bucket. Oh, what to do! Just like Liza, we need to come up with something to patch our hearts. And here is where we put some work into the adventure of aging. Don't allow excuses to get in the way of a joy-filled path on your aging journey. Excuses are so easy to fall back on, but they just aren't going to patch your 'bucket.'

So what might get in the way of a strong, reliable patch?

And I know there are many concerns on your list. There might be many reasons why life has its challenges, but it is important to search for solutions that will put just a bit of sunshine into the day. And you say, "That is easy for you to say!" and you are right. But remember Liza…she wasn't going to get anywhere if she didn't find some way to mend that bucket. Don't give up. Don't quit. Don't focus on the impossible. Even mending with bubble bum got me home!

Lord,

There are so many things to consider as I grow older. I laugh a bit when I think of the picture of me with a hole in my bucket, but do you know…that is how I feel sometimes.

Lord,

Some days I seem to walk to get that bucket of water, getting tired just thinking about the trip back. And then to find that I have lost half of what was in my bucket. Do I patch that bucket or get a new one?

Lord,

I think sometimes we try so hard to patch what is wrong with our life. We feel lonely, and we try to patch that feeling with something that just doesn't work. Sometimes we experience financial worries at our age and try to pretend that everything is okay. Pretending just doesn't work!

Lord,

If I do get a new bucket, will you keep an eye on me so that I take proper care of this new purchase? I will keep it clean, store it in a safe place and use it carefully. That's kind of the way I need to think about this ol' body of mine. I can't go out and buy a new one, so I must take care of what I have.

Lord,

Help me keep my body healthy. Help me take care of myself rather than pretend that all is well. Those are the times when I need to remember to reach out to others who are going to understand why there is a hole in my heart.

Lord,

It's my heart that ends up with the hole in it. Sometimes the love and energy, and inspiration have just leaked out of that hole, and I don't know what to do. If you help me with the patching job, I know that it is going to hold. I know that with your help, there will be no more pretend patches. Thanks for the help.

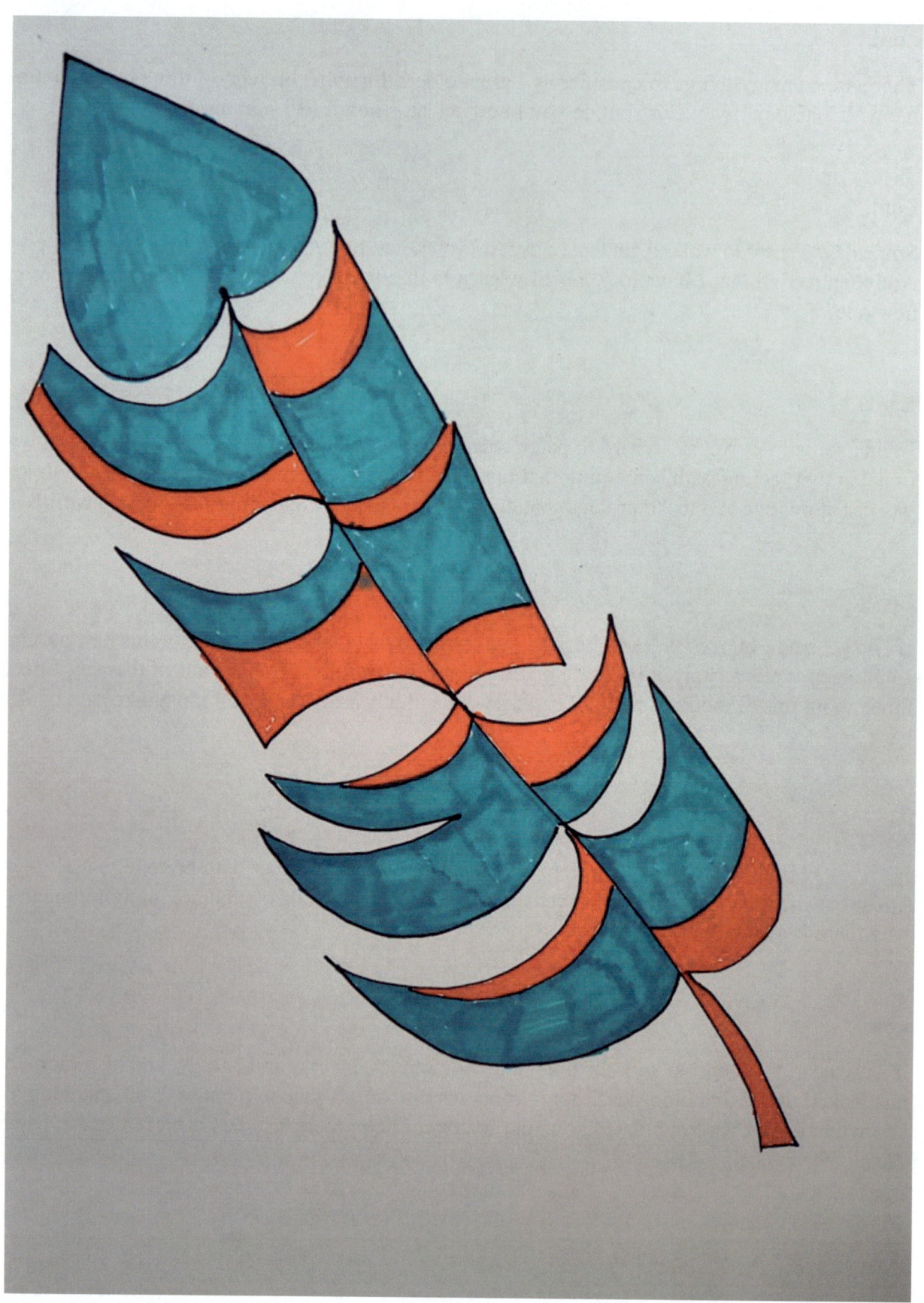

GOING HOME...

I've been a grown adult for many years, living far from the home where I grew up. Pay attention to stories from your friends, and I would tend to think that even though they may live far from the home where they grew up, they still refer to it as 'home'! Home was a beginning. However blessed we were with the way in which we began our lives or how challenged and trauma filled those years might have been, it remains as a place called 'home.'

Years ago, I made a video of my hometown community...actually, one for my home as well as that of my husband. I wandered everywhere, talking with people and recording places that had been meaningful to us. There were the old grain elevators where my father hauled his truckloads of wheat. Main Street had lost several of the business places, but there was still the grocery on the corner, the furniture store across the street, and the pharmacy way down the block. I could remember being a part of that community, and with the video, I had memories in hand.

Remembering and memories.

There were changes...so many changes. The streets had been widened. The old elementary school had been torn down. People I had known no longer lived in the houses that had been so familiar. Here and there, new buildings had appeared, which hopefully meant that there was still life in this little town.

Changes.

I smile when I think of how many things I have forgotten. Just today, I was working on something and left my desk to walk into the kitchen for something I needed. Just a few steps, and there I was...what was it that I was looking for? I forget the day of the week, what it was that I needed at the grocery, returning the dishes to a friend who had shared a meal with us...and on and on the list could go. I can talk myself into being upset with forgetting, but I think it is quite normal. Remember my overflowing water tub by the garden...it's my overflowing life with too much to remember.

Forgetting is so frustrating.

I had been a part of this community in the yesterdays of my life. Even though I no longer lived in northern Minnesota, there were things happening today that I could relate to. High school friends had chosen to live their lives in that area. I smiled at photos that were posted on Facebook. School reunions. There were still connections. But as for tomorrow. The part of my life was moving on elsewhere. I could remember, but I no longer was an actual part of that part of my life. I was growing older, stepping into tomorrow but not knowing what tomorrow would bring. My life had been a process. One place. One step. Growing through all the stages of life.

Yesterday, today, and tomorrow.

With age comes certain limitations, things we no longer do unless we carefully plan how it will all take place. Driving a long distance becomes difficult. Air travel is no longer a sure thing. I can't imagine spending a night in the airport because of changes in schedules. Visits to family a long distance away take on a whole new aspect. Oh, I remember when my friend and relative gave me a hug as we were leaving their home. She was struggling with a significant health issue, and we both knew that the future was questionable. With tears, she hugged me and said, "I might not see you again." Those words make saying 'goodbye' so painful.

It's life. I might not see you again. I can't change the circumstances. She can't ignore her advancing health concerns. All we can manage together is the reality of the moment. We are saying goodbye.

I am able to determine when spring is just around the corner. Even grocery stores have racks that hold vegetable and flower seeds. Some stores like to display their live plants outdoors, tempting my eyes as I drive by. And then there are always the extraordinarily tall stacks of munch.

If I choose to garden beginning with seeds, there is definitely preparation. Potting soil, containers, and a safe place where the seeds will germinate. And then, one day, a tiny piece of green pops up through the dirt. The work isn't over. Now it is time to transplant those green things into the real garden.

The seeds mature and are ready for their summer home. Carefully they are transplanted and cared for. Being on guard for creatures who would love to make a salad of my garden is equally as important as all the preparation I have gone through to get my seeds ready to grow. The plants eventually grow strong and tall, promising a bountiful crop as autumn comes near.

How tempting to pick a ripe tomato as I walk through an autumn garden. You can smell the freshness just walking by. I'll pick a couple of green beans and eat a couple before they even make their way into the kitchen. Watching pumpkins and squash grow and take shape is as much fun as planning. It's soon time to harvest. Everything tastes better when it comes fresh from the garden.

All the garden work is completed for the season. Pumpkins have been cooked and made into puree for pumpkin pie. Corn has been removed from the cob and placed in baggies to be frozen for a winter meal. Green beans are canned, and the cucumbers have been magically turned into pickles.

After a few days of hard work, the garden is cleaned up, for the soil is ready for another new season…next spring. Maybe I will add just a bit of fertilizer to encourage good growth.

The seasons change, and each season has a purpose. Spring begins with new plans, and winter brings time to rest. And in between, there is time to enjoy a pumpkin pie.

And so goes life. I mentioned the sweet newborns and the need for parents to learn how this little creature will flourish with special loving care. Summer days come as that new baby grows as fast as those seeds you planted in that rich soil. Summer for this young adult is a time of learning and exploring and eventually stepping into the autumn of life. The seasons pass quickly.

Autumn brings opportunities and growth, and adventures. A sense of pride with accomplishments, and then the seasons change again as we consider all that has been accomplished. Job completed. Children raised. Success with adventures that were explored. Work well done.

Work well done. Time to rest. Your significant responsibilities have been achieved. Planning for a day off has turned into free time whenever and wherever I may choose to use it. It's time to be still, to rest, to ponder what's ahead.

Looking back, it's remembering a lifetime of experiences as well as forgetting a few things along the way. Life over the years has brought considerable change. Change in your personal life as well as with family and friends and the work in which you have been involved, in your community and the world.

And there has been growth. The seasons have made you into who you have become. Spring, summer, and autumn saw seasons of growth and harvest. A new season is upon us…winter and a bit of rest. I know what I have done yesterday. My todays have been used, one at a time, and tomorrow is opening a new path for me. But…it's my unique journey. You and I can walk together, hold each other's hand, but our paths may not be the same. Change. Change again. You wave goodbye to me as your path turns off in a different direction.

And it's time to ponder the quietness, the freedom from a schedule, and the change in responsibilities. It's time to soak up the 'golden' part of what people call the golden years.

This is our season for those of us who are receiving social security and sleeping a bit later in the morning. It's our time to explore a new adventure, whatever that might be. It's our time to sit back, remembering yesterday and contemplating just how tomorrow might look.

Oh, I know that not everyone sees aging as a gift. I know there are challenges with health or relationships, loss, or finances. That's a tough part of growing older, but… and there is a 'but' to that situation.

Somehow, I need to be open to reaching out and accepting support. Somehow, I need to search deep within and dare to explore my aging attitude. No, I don't have answers to these difficult concerns, the realities of aging, but I do know it is possible to be pliable enough to consider those inevitable changes. Change may be difficult. It might involve my physical mobility, self-care, leaving a familiar home, or experiencing the loss of a loved one. I can learn! I am not going to give in to what it is that I can no longer do. I'm not going to turn my back on an offer of loving care from someone.

Back to my stories. Do you remember falling off your bike when the training wheels were off? Do you remember struggling with a sport when others on the team performed like Olympic athletes? Do you remember not being able to learn that crazy new dance everyone in high school just loved?

But even when our knees were scraped or our egos damaged, we moved on. We left the season of childhood and stepped into the world of responsibilities. Maybe it was seeking a place of employment or a new area in which to live. Maybe it was the 24/7 responsibility of caring for a young family or your aging parents. So many things to do as you maintain your own life. Finding a sense of joy and satisfaction in who you were becoming seemed to be quite a task.

Summer had arrived.

Autumn had sure signs – cool evenings, changes of color in the leaves, kids back in school, and vacations were now a good memory. One day, after what seemed like many years, a thought came to your mind. It might be time to slow down and explore another path. Can it be true – all these years and now, I have been seeing changes in my life that gradually have brought me to winter, a season of stillness, gentleness, or quietness. Oh, I know there may be a passing storm, but that's when we learn to hunker down in a safe and healthy place with those who love and care for us.

In the quietness, we consider tomorrow and prepare ourselves for this new season. The seasons of spring, summer, and autumn…and now winter has brought – and will bring – blessings and challenges and roots across our path, forgetting and remembering, growing and changing…saying goodbye on our journey home.

But what is the most important thing to remember about the seasons we have explored and will explore…never for a minute are we traveling alone. Always remember that the cloud that guides us during the light and the fire that will follow to provide guidance in the dark will always be there. That's something important to remember! We continue to learn and grow. We make changes and adapt. We are blessed, and we won't give up.

Lord,

I have been here a long time. It's been good. Thank you for the adventure.

I have been here a long time and have done a lot of things right, but there have been things where I really messed up. I rejoice for the good in my life, and I have an empty place when I am reminded of my mistakes.

Yesterday, today, and tomorrow. That's a long time. But, do you know, I would like to stay here for a long time. I want to go places I haven't been, see things I haven't seen and do things I haven't done. I want to watch our grandson grow into an adult. I wonder where his life will take him. I want to know that our family will continue on a safe path as they eventually age.

I want to see the world become a safer place to live. I want to see people caring for each other rather than using violence to solve problems. I want to see solutions to cures for serious health issues. I want to see mental health become a manageable concern.

Lord,

There is just so much I want, but I have to leave that all in your hands. Somehow, I know that as much as I want to be a part of all those desires, you are going to care for your people in this world just as you have for generations and generations.

So, I have been thinking about coming to your house. You did promise that you would have a room for me. I don't know when our getting together will take place, but I know we will both be ready.

And all that I ask is I prepare for my journey to your house is that you continue to care for all that is precious to me on this earth. I think you for that.

It's been quite a journey. I have been a part of so many life changes during my years on this earth. Hopes and joys. Challenges. Concerns. Laughing and crying. Just plain living. It's been good.

Put that big rocking chair on your front porch, and I will be eager for a time to fill my soul. I do appreciate your warm welcome.

I'll be seeing you soon. Keep me safe on the journey. Thanks for the gift of life you have shared with me.

One last story…

And Perry shares: My wife and I are moving from the home in which we have lived for over fifty years. Our two wonderful daughters have but rarely had a Christmas anywhere else. And for a quarter of a century, our marvelous sons-in-law or our loving and beloved six grandchildren have not missed a Christmas with us.

This year as I was taking down the faux-evergreen wreaths which had decorated our house's columns and removing the faux-fir boa which had decorated our living room mantel, I realized that there was no need to box these things up carefully to be reused next year. Before this moment actually came, I used to contemplate it with a hesitantly peripheral sort of vision and thought it would be truly painful. Not at all. There was, rather, a sense of the simplification of things – or rather, a liberation.

As our daughters and their families bade us farewell for that last time, leaving the 'old house,' there were some tears and, more slightly, some stiff faces which evidence deep and possible tear-producing emotions. All to be expected.

But what was unexpected was the query from the youngest of our grandchildren, a wonderful sixteen-year-old boy, "Hey guys, why the tears? Grandma and Grandaddy will be moving to OUR neighborhood. They won't be seven hours away anymore! That's a great thing!"

And so, it is….

And so is every age of the miraculous gift of life, even maybe especially the aging part of the life gift. The circle of life.

This is a journey where we can't rearrange the direction forward. There is no reverse button. We are traveling together! It's a journey with trials and frustrations, confusion and wonder, love and deep joy. So many memories and stories. As the circle begins to come together, it is becoming a journey of peace, knowing that we are traveling with a loving God who reminds us:

"Welcome home. You have traveled well."

And I responded: **"God, the door was open, thus I entered. I put my shoes by the door. It's good to be home!"**

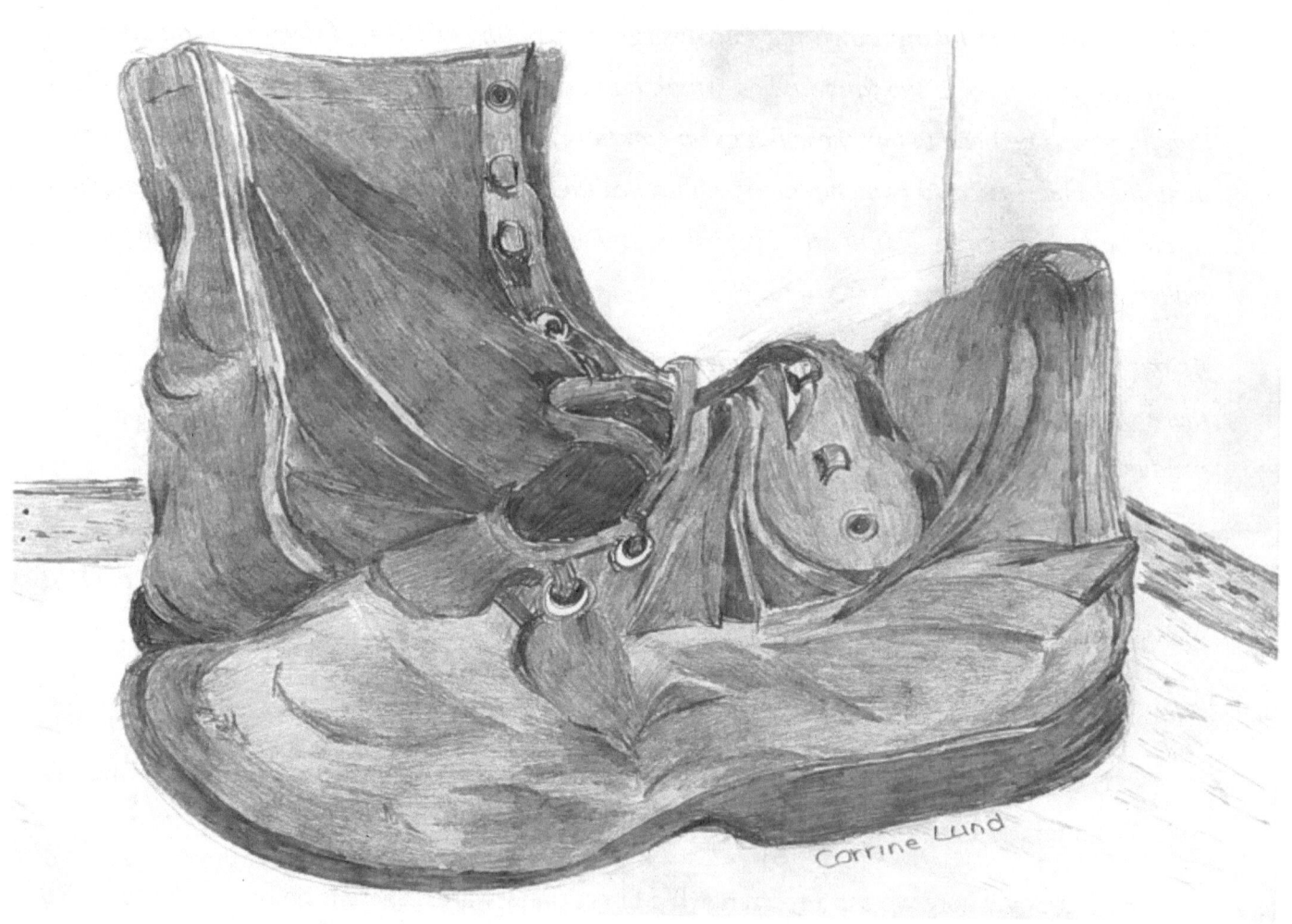

So, I am not sure how many endings a book can have…but I have a final ending. My husband and I just watched the movie "A Man Named Otto"[1], starring Tom Hanks. And yes, we shed some tears throughout this amazing movie. There is an ending message beyond the ending of the movie, and I feel that I need to end my book with the same sentiments.

Growing older is not a piece of cake. Growing older with challenges is not a piece of cake. Growing older alone is not a piece of cake. What I am saying is that many of us are going to grow older in one form or another. What is important is that we are there for each other. We are there to support each other through all the different paths we will take. We are there to support each other when we celebrate together and cry together.

Keep your heart open to what others are experiencing as they are walking the path of growing older. We can't do this alone. We did not come into this world alone. We did not learn and grow alone, and we cannot leave this world alone. Keep your heart open to what others who are growing older are experiencing, and keep your heart open to those who are going to be there for you as you walk the journey of growing older.

Thank you, Otto, for sharing your journey of challenges and love. It's a blessing to have a 'heart that is too big"! The journey is not a piece of cake…but we can do it!

When I wrote *God blessed them for the journey*, I wanted the reader to be actively involved in my book, whether it was in the words I shared to the various activities I suggested. Well, I have now completed my second book. Amazing!

It seems I have created an ending to this collection of stories several times, and here I am again. There is something new on my plate as I send my manuscript off to the publisher. My husband has just had an episode with his heart, and we are both grateful beyond words that he received the care he needed and is on the 'road to recovery.' All the aspects of aging that I have shared throughout this book were a part of our days at the Ross Heart Center/Ohio State University. (And here is another smile…so many of the medical people who were in charge of

---

the most critical of situations looked to be 'just kids! Of course, they weren't but thank you to the younger generation for caring for us, the older generation!)

So many people our age struggle with concerns related to heart issues as they are growing older. There was equipment that we could not begin to understand. Some of the procedures were so new that they were not yet available in the day-to-day world of medicine. In fact, we came home with a huge box of that very equipment, and my husband is not part of a study related to yet another new medical advancement.

Dare I say that there are experiences in these challenges that are extremely interesting! We learned and learned…and then would forget and would need to ask questions, over and over. Not once did we feel as though we were traveling alone. We spent days being supported and guided on all sides. People were caring and helpful, and after being home just overnight, there had already been a telephone call asking if there was anything we needed after leaving the hospital.

It's going to happen, my Friends. We are going to experience life changes – fun and exciting as well as frightening and challenging. How many times have I encouraged you to be open to all those around you who love and care for you? My family has just lived through what could have been one of the chapters of this book.

And now I say to you, the readers, thank you for sharing this journey with me. Take/ make time to become involved in your journey of aging.

Thoughts to Ponder as I Grow Older

I'm On a Journey

No matter what my age, each day brings a new adventure.

Not Getting the Message

Even though I recognize changes in my body, I don't pay attention.

Security In Being Uncomfortable

Sometimes I find it easier to not make changes.

Now What Do I Do?

How did I become older so quickly?

Will It Help to Think About This Process?

I will take some time today to just think about aging.

I Don't Like How This All Feels To Me.

I can laugh on the outside, but inside, I don't like it.

How is My Attitude?

Maybe it is time to consider my attitude toward aging.

Preparing For the Journey

How does one 'prepare' for growing older?

But I Don't Know How To Prepare!

I will remember to reach out to others for guidance.

Newsflash!

Guess what? I'm not on this journey alone!

Learning

Sit quietly and allow yourself to be open to learning.

Being Overwhelmed!

Sometimes it is exciting to learn new things, but on other days, I feel like I am the bowling pins and the ball is coming down the alley.

Dark Shadows in the Future

I'm enjoying life at this moment, but what if there is an unknown in the future?

My Feelings Jump Around Everywhere

Is it normal to be so confused about growing older…and a bit frightened. Why are my feelings so out of control? One day I am up and the next day I am down in the dumps

Experiences

I don't need to reinvent the world, but what can I do to shine a positive light on my day-to-day adventures?

Remember… I Am Not Alone

Sometimes I just think about myself, which is not helpful or healthy.

Remembering Others

Time to think of ways in which I can reach out to help others

I Wish You Had Not Said That

People mean well, but sometimes, I just don't want to be reminded of what I can no longer do.

Don't Put Off What I Need to Do Today

I don't always have the energy – so let's get this job completed today.

Don't Worry About Tomorrow

I will do today what seems to be right for me, and I won't think about tomorrow.

Light-Hearted Banter Takes Away the Miseries of Daily Life – Always remember To Lighten Up.

It doesn't add anything to my day to be grumpy…lighten up.

Becoming Involved in the 'Process'

Growing older doesn't happen in an instant...How can I become involved in the process, one day at a time?

I Really Am Learning About This Aging Thing...

Through all my aging experiences, it is good to know that it is possible to develop and grow, even as I become older.

Enjoy the View

I might not be able to climb to the top of the mountain, but the scenery can be quite lovely in the valley.

Be Patient...

    Be Honest...

        Be Accepting...

            Be Courageous...

                Be Ready for the Unknown...

                    Be Ready for the Known

I can do this… and so can you!

You have gone through the month, day by day. Find a journal or a notebook where you can continue thinking about your adventures as you grow older, whether you are having a cloudy day or if the sun is shining. One day at a time in this process of growing older is all you need to manage. I am pleased that you have joined me on this journey, even for just this day.

Philippians 4: 12 – 13

I know what it is to be in need, and I know what it is to have plenty. I have learned the secret of being content in any and every situation, whether well-fed or hungry, whether living in plenty or in want. I can do everything through God, who gives me strength.

How amazing is the sound of grace

Amazing grace

How sweet is the sound. Sweeter than anything I could ever imagine. I once was lost and confused, but now I seem to feel I know where it is that I am going.

Sometimes I am overwhelmed by the world in which I live…a world so busy that it makes my head spin. There is so much to learn even as I am growing older. I want to just stop and say…*Enough!*

Amazing

God Is

Hmm, an incomplete sentence with a totally complete thought.

God Is.

And I am, and you are…we all are complete in knowing who we are. The shaping of a clay pot cannot be separated from the artist, nor can I, a child of God's creation, be separated from my Creator.

Amazing.

So, I continue walking the steps of growing older, knowing there is still a purpose for my life. How do I know what that purpose might be, even at my age? God made a promise to me that not for one moment would God leave my side. In the creation of millions and billions of plans, God promised me that I would have individual attention in order to complete my journey.

Amazing

Sometimes It is a challenge to find my way. The dark seems to overtake the light…even though the dark can seem overpowering, I will continue to search for the spaces of light in my life.

Sometimes I feel as though I am lost…

But I have been found all along the way, in and out of one day, after another.

Amazing

Grace

This is all an amazing gift, and I just need to be still and listen, pay attention, and be open to guidance.

I will be still and listen as I live my life, one day at a time.

How sweet that can be.

How gentle and safe.

How calming and reassuring.

In my younger years, I was too busy. Now I have time to 'be still and listen"!

Amazing

This is for you and for me.

BUT I've never kept a journal! → It's just thinking with pen and paper.

AND there are NO Rules!

↓ you need...
- a place where I can see my thoughts
- a place where I can pause and reflect
- a place where I can be in the 'quiet'
- a place to be creative

AND THEN YOU CAN BEGIN!

★ Get out your paper and pencil

? Did I experience anything unique today?
? Was there worry or concern in my day?
? Am I thankful or needy?
? What has filled my heart to overflowing?

• You get the idea... It's about moving out of your head and listening to your heart!

The Writing Process

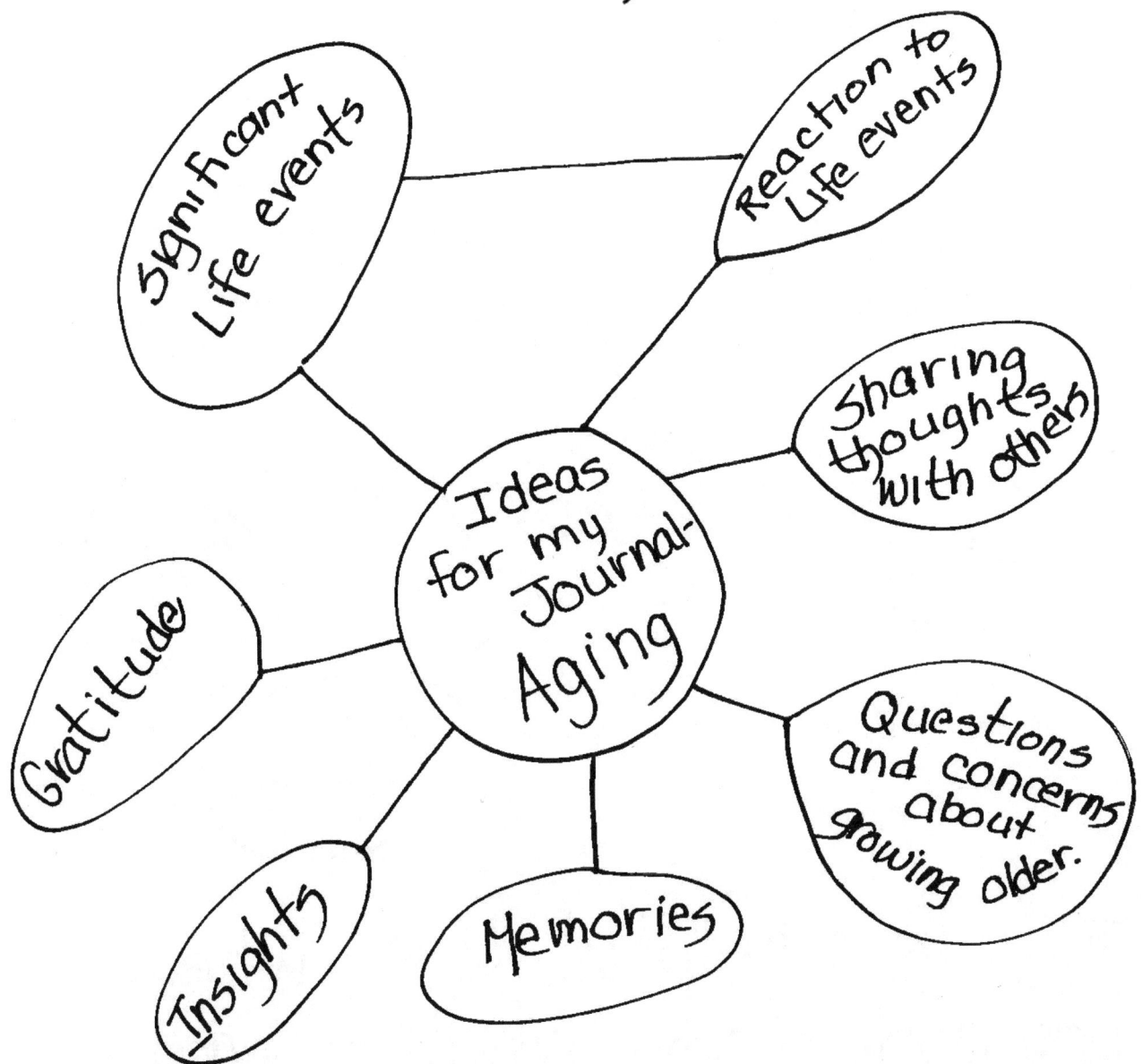

Just write! Don't be critical.
Be honest! Be yourself.
Write what you feel.

Webbing with the W's

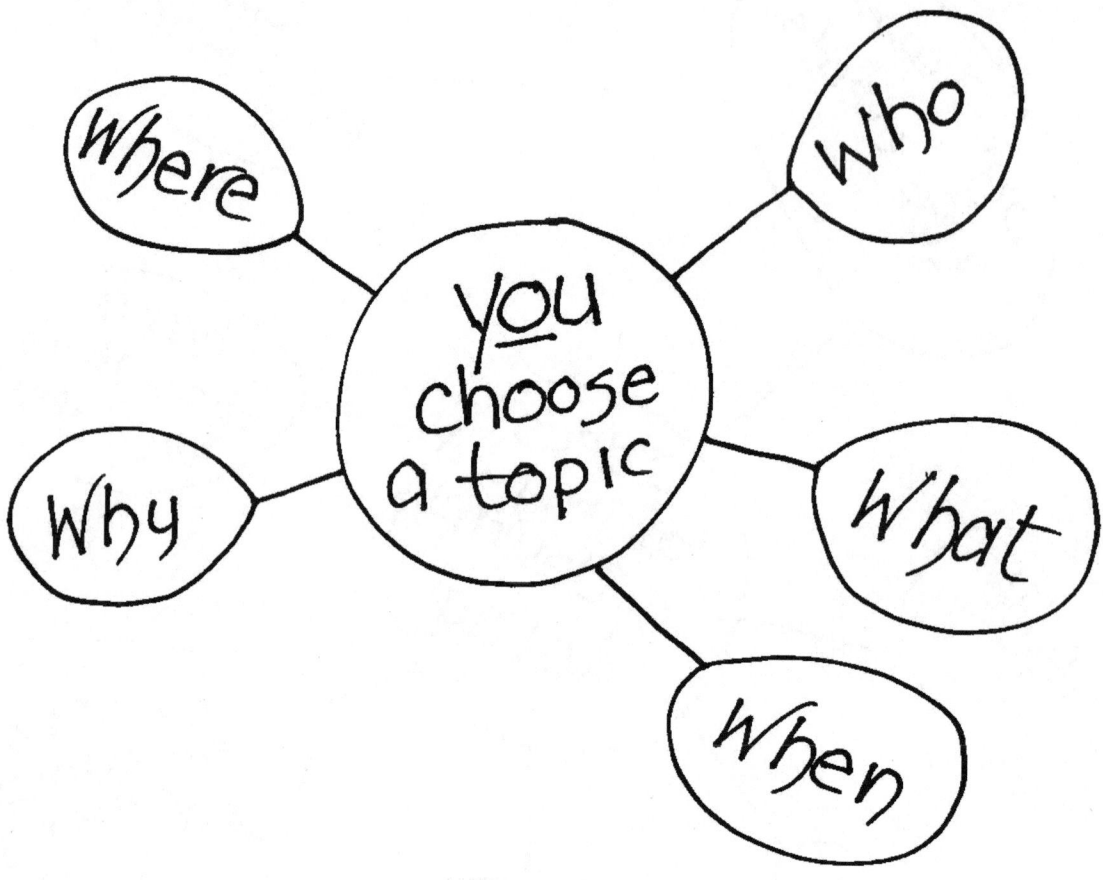

This is a helpful tool when you don't know what to write. Begin in the middle with a topic - something on your mind. Move out to the W's and write.

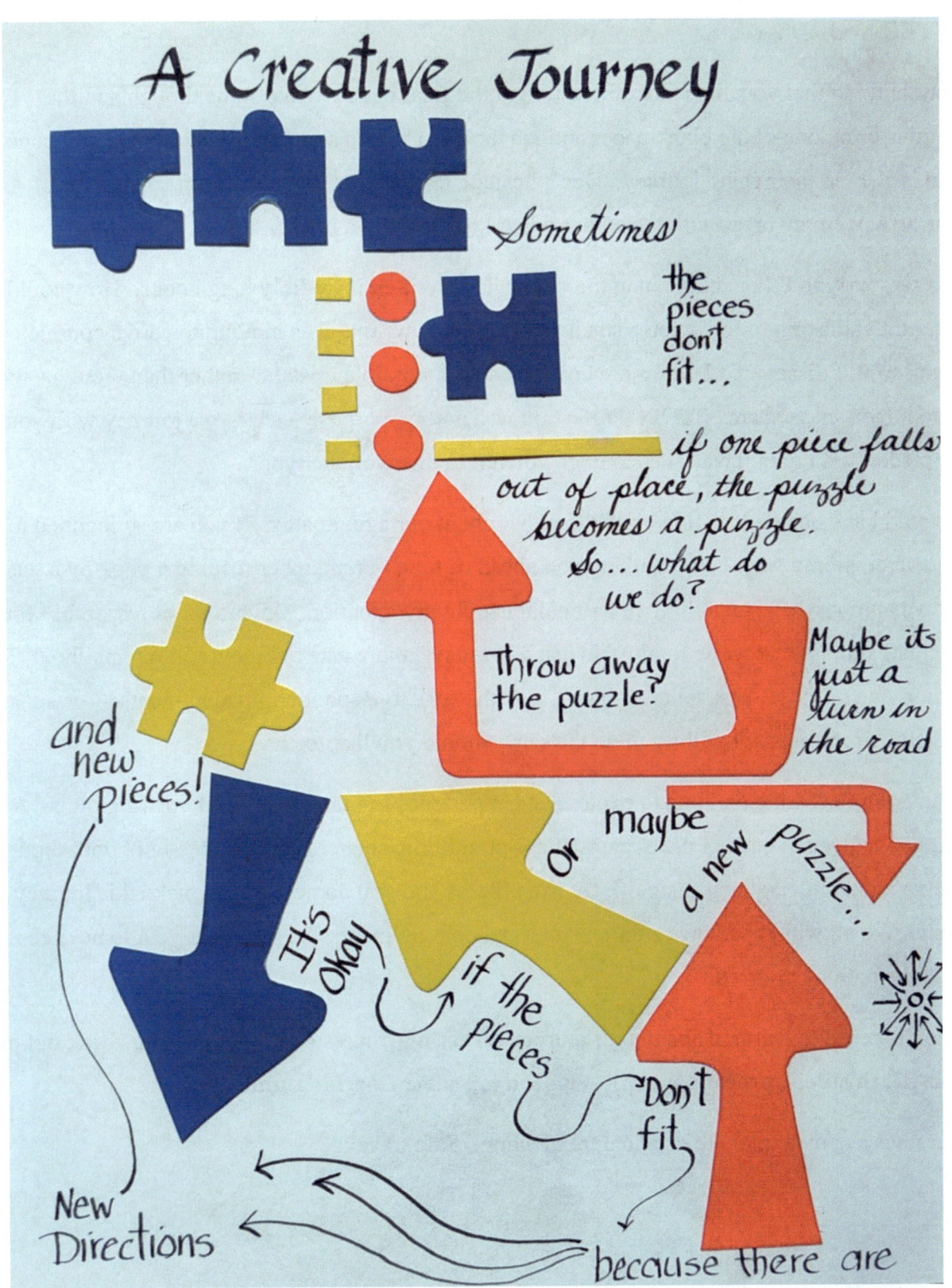

AFTER-WORDS

I am thinking that you, the reader, have turned the final pages, wrote some thoughts in the margins or on one of the blank pages and maybe even shared some of my ideas with someone who is also on their aging journey. Don't hesitate to write in this book. I am so in favor of sharing any empty areas with the author when I am reading a book.

As I was writing I thought about authors who have written incredibly long books. How could they edit and begin to find even a small error? As my writing was moving toward a completed manuscript, I discovered I was more concerned with possible mistakes rather than thoughts that were important to share. STOP! Perfection was not my purpose – sharing a journey with you the reader was my purpose! I encourage you not to dwell on the typos.

It would have been interesting to talk together about our aging paths. If you are so inclined to send an email my way, I am thanking you ahead of time. I remember reading a book by a well-known author where something in particular caught my attention. After a bit of research, I found an email address and wrote to him. In just a few days, there was a response in my mailbox. This author, one of those 'best seller authors', took the time to respond to my comments. I was…and still am…impressed. I will try to do the same should you like to chat.

Thank you for taking the time to explore and experience my thoughts about growing older. It is going to happen to each of us, circumstances permitting, sooner or later. One important thought I leave with you…aging is a significant life process and you do not need to make this journey alone. We all will experience a unique journey…but no matter the situation, you do not need to walk the path by yourself.

I look forward to learning about your journey **(creatingprocess@gmail.com)** and check out my **website. thislifeisaproces.com** or just type in my name **Corrine Lund**

Blessings as you explore this adventure of aging. Safe travels!

About the Author

I would rather write and work in my studio than tend to laundry! I suppose as one ages and retirement takes the place of a regular work schedule, I can let some of those routine tasks rest on the back burner while I enjoy my creating. If I had known, at an early age, that this was to be my life journey, I would have said, "You must be kidding!" What an amazing surprise this path has been.

My years growing up, being a wife and mother, educator, and creator, have all come together to make me the person I am. And now, after many years of living, I have completed my second book and am ready to change pen and paper for more time to weave and draw. Change is good!

One never gets too old to continue the journey – wherever your path may have taken you. My path is not what I had expected, and I hope that I am going to be able to 'mess around' in my studio for some time yet. As I said in the book, "I have definitely explored the autumn season of my life and am well into winter." But…growing up in northern Minnesota, I never did mind winter. I am going to continue with that same philosophy as I create, watching snowflakes cover my sidewalk, but I am certainly going to keep the shovel handy so that winter doesn't prevent me from continuing my journey.

From our first breath, life changes every day. Don't be afraid to take the next step. Aging is an expected part of the journey all of us experience. Don't be afraid. You aren't traveling alone!

Made in the USA
Columbia, SC
08 January 2025